Cantonese
phrasebook

Kam Y Lau

Cantonese Phrasebook
  1st edition

Published by
Lonely Planet Publications
Head Office: PO Box 617, Hawthorn, Vic 3122, Australia
Branches: PO Box 2001A, Berkeley, CA 94702, USA
10 Barley Mow Passage, Chiswick, London W4 4PH, UK
71 bis rue du Cardinal Lemoine, 75005 Paris, France

Printed by
Colorcraft Ltd, Hong Kong

This Book
This book was written by Kam Y Lau. Sally Steward edited the book and
Caroline Williamson assisted in proofreading. Illustrations and cover
design were by Tamsin Wilson, and Ann Jeffree was responsible for design.
For their assistance and support, the author would like to thank his family,
especially his daughter, Sally. Thanks also to Felicia Zhang, Diane Douglas
and John Hsu for their invaluable advice.

Published
 · June 1994

National Library of Australia Cataloguing in Publication Data

Lau, Kam Y
  Cantonese Phrasebook.

  ISBN 0 86442 217 2

  1. Cantonese dialects - Conversation and phrase books - English.
  I. Title. (Series: Lonely Planet language survival kit).

495.17

Contents

Introduction

Cantonese is one of the five major dialects of the Chinese language (the mother tongue often referred to as *hanyu* by the Chinese) although it is only spoken by 6% of the *hanyu*-speaking population worldwide. The five dialects are *putonghua* (Mandarin, the official language of China), *yue* (Cantonese), *wu*, *min* and *kejia*. These dialects are, however, sufficiently different from each other to be more commonly referred to as individual languages.

Although *putonghua* is the official Chinese language, it has a history of only around 700 to 800 years, compared to Cantonese which has a history of over 2000 years. Cantonese has retained most of the characteristics of the classic *hanyu*, such as the clipped sound of words ending with *-p*, *-t* and *-k*, and the *-m*. It is also the only dialect in *hanyu* to have retained its complete series of tones.

The major Cantonese-speaking areas include most of Guangdong (Canton), the southern part of Guangxi, Hong Kong and Macau. It is the language of most overseas Chinese.

Cantonese has been enriched over time by the addition of many words from other languages, resulting from centuries of contact with many European and South-East Asian countries. Canton, known to the Chinese as Guangzhou, used to be the place where Cantonese was considered to be at its purest, but due to the influence of Hong Kong's media and pop music throughout the Cantonese-speaking areas, Hong Kong Cantonese has become the more acceptable, or even official, standard of speaking. Basically now, Cantonese can be described as an old language with a new life.

It's hard to write every word spoken because Cantonese is a very oral dialect. Many of the words used are slang and cannot be written. However the language that *is* written is written in the same script as Mandarin.

This phrasebook is based on contemporary Hong Kong Cantonese although vocabulary specific to mainland China is included, and all words and phrases included are polite and colloquial – the sort of words you'll encounter as you travel.

The word 'Chinese' used in this book means all things Chinese, including Cantonese, while the word 'Cantonese' means specifically all things Cantonese, or from a Cantonese-speaking background. The signs at the end of various chapters in the book, such as the one below, show ancient script characters, from which the modern Cantonese characters have derived.

Stand together

Pronunciation

Pronunciation described in this chapter is based on the Cantonese spoken in Hong Kong, as this is increasingly the most commonly heard. Some tones, vowels, consonants and vocabulary vary within the various Cantonese-speaking regions; however most Cantonese-speaking people can understand Hong Kong Cantonese.

If you're unsure of the pronunciation, ask a local to pronounce the words for you. Even if they don't understand the phonetic system used in this book, most will be able to read the Chinese characters. Hearing the correct sounds and relating them to characters is obviously the best way to learn. And if you have difficulty getting the message across at any time, you can simply point to the appropriate Chinese characters.

Young people nowadays often don't pronounce certain consonants, or they change one consonant to another. For example, *ng-* is often ignored and not pronounced at all. Thus *ngō jàu* (Australia) becomes *ō jàu*, and *ngőh* (I) becomes *őh*. Another common practice is the dropping of the consonant -*w*- in *kw*- and *gw*-, as in *gwóng dùng wá* (Cantonese language) which becomes *góng dùng wá*, and *kwōng* (a mine) becoming *kōng*. Finally, young people often mix the *n* and the *l*, as in *nai* (mud) which becomes *lai*, and *ngőh ngōi néî* (I love you), becoming *őh ōi léî*.

Tones

Tone is the decisive factor when judging whether your Cantonese is good or not; it's also the most difficult aspect of the Cantonese language to learn, which will probably come as no surprise.

In total there more than ten tones in Cantonese, including the variations, however, they may be simplified into six basic tones.

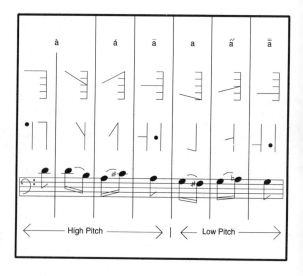

This phrasebook adopts a tonic sign system in which the six basic tones are described in terms of a pitch scale of one to five. Level five on the pitch scale is the highest and level one the lowest. The basic tones are divided into two groups: high pitch and low pitch.

High Pitch Group

Tone number one has the highest pitch and is given a five on the pitch scale. Words with this tone have either a clipped sound (refer to the Clipped Pitch section in this chapter), a long, lingering pitch or a sound that drops slightly. These words are indicated by the falling symbol (ˋ) on the first vowel.

The second tone starts on three on the pitch scale, and rises to five. Words with the second tone are marked by a rising symbol (ˊ) on the first vowel.

The third is a levelled tone and has a clipped sound, or it could have a lingering sound. Words with the third tone are shown by the line over the first vowel.

fòo	*fóo*	*fōo*
husband	tiger	wealthy

Low Pitch Group

The fourth tone starts on two on the pitch scale and drops to one. Words with the fourth tone have no symbols.

The fifth tone also starts on two but rises to three on the pitch level. Words with the fifth tone are marked by the symbol (˝) on the first vowel.

The sixth tone is a levelled tone and has a clipped sound, or it may stay on level two on the pitch scale. Words with the sixth tone are shown by double lines over the first vowel.

foo	*fő̋o*	*fō͞o*
to lean	woman	owe

Clipped Pitch

Cantonese words ending with the consonants *p*, *t* and *k* have a clipped sound, similar to words with a silent letter in English, such as the word 'climb'. The letter is almost ready to be pronounced but is stopped intentionally before a sound is made.

For example, although *màt* (what) and *màn* (mosquito) start on the ame pitch, the endings are different. The *màt* has a higher but short clipped sound whereas *màn* has the same pitch but the sound is sustained for a longer period of time. Words ending with *p*, *t* or *k* normally only belong to the first, third and sixth tones.

Consonants

The following is a list of consonants you will come across in phonetic Cantonese; most you are already familiar with.

b, ch, d, f, g, gw, h, j, k, kw, l, m, n, ng, p, s, t, w, y

Vowels

Different textbooks adopt different systems when dealing with vowels in Cantonese. In the author's view, the system used in Sidney Lau's textbook, *Elementary Cantonese* (Government Printer, Hong Kong) is the most appropriate system for this phrasebook.

There are many variations when pronouncing English, so the sounds described here are based on standard British English to provide some uniformity. In the following list, the single **a** is a short sound and the double **aa** is long.

Vowel Combination	Sound in English	Example		Meaning
a	rather	*fà*	花	flower
aai	find	*gàai*	街	street
ai	lie	*gài*	雞	chicken
aau	loud	*bàau*	包	to pack

au	now	*chàu*	秋	autumn
aam	**farm**	*sàam*	三	three
am	**come**	*sàm*	心	heart
aan	**aunt**	*sàan*	山	mountain
an	**fun**	*fàn*	分	minute
aang	'arn' + 'ng'	*sàang*	生	birth
ang	**sung**	*dàng*	燈塔	lamp
aap	**carp**	*tāap*	塔	tower
ap	**cup**	*sàp*	濕	wet
aat	**art**	*bāat*	八	eight
at	**cut**	*yàt*	一	one
aak	**ark**	*bāak*	百	hundred
ak	**luck**	*bàk*	北	north
e	let	*chè*	車	car
ek	**neck**	*tēk*	踢	to kick
eng	**length**	*gēng*	鏡	mirror
ei	**pay**	*fèi*	飛	to fly
euh	**fur**	*hèuh*	靴	boot
eung	'urn' + 'ng'	*hèung*	香	fragrance
euk	**jerk**	*gēuk*	腳	leg
i	me	*sì*	獅	lion
iu	'ee' + 'ew'	*sìu*	燒	to burn
im	**him**	*tìm*	添	to add
in	**in**	*tìn*	天	sky
ing	**king**	*sìng*	星	star
ip	**lip**	*jĭp*	接	to receive
it	**it**	*jĭt*	節	festival
ik	**sick**	*sìk*	識	to know

o	go	*dò*	刀	knife
oh	**or**	*sòh*	梳	comb
oi	toy	*hòi*	開	to open
ok	lock	*gwōk*	國	country
on	on	*gòn*	干	dry
ong	long	*fòng*	方	square
oo	foo	*fòo*	夫	husband
ooi	'oo' + 'ee'	*bòoi*	杯	cup
oon	moon	*bòon*	搬	to move
oot	foot	*fōot*	闊	wide
ot	hot	*gōt*	割	to cut
ue	like 'ew'	*yúe*	魚	fish
uen	like 'ewn'	*jùen*	磚	brick
uet	flute	*sūet*	雪	snow
ui	'oy' + 'ee'	*kùi*	區	area
un	very short 'oo' + 'n'	*chùn*	春	spring
ut	short **put**	*chùt*	出	out
ung	very short 'oo' + 'ng'	*jùng*	鐘	bell
uk	cook	*jùk*	竹	bamboo
m	**mmm**	*m*	唔	not
ng	ra**ng**	*nǧ*	五	five

Here are some sayings, which use all the tones, and in tonic order:

- *tèng góng fōh; chai séung hŏk*　　聽講課;齊上學
  'to listen, to lecture, lessons; together, to attend, school' –
  this literally means 'going to school together and listening
  to the lectures'.

- *jùng góng ngō; cham mǎai mǎai*   中港澳;尋買賣
  'China, Hong Kong, Macau; to seek, to buy, to sell' – this stands for China, Hong Kong and Macau joining forces to attract businesses.

- *gùng héi! gùng héi!*   恭喜!恭喜!
  Congratulations! Congratulations! – you should now have no trouble speaking Cantonese.

Stand

Grammar

The Chinese language (including Cantonese) is fundamentally different from many other languages. Every character bears its own meaning and its own, one-syllable sound.

Sentence Structure

The word order in sentences is very similar to the English order of subject-verb-object. The function of words relies on their position in a sentence. For example the simple sentence 'I love you' follows exactly the same order in Cantonese, *ngőh ngōi néî* and, like English, would take on a different meaning if the position of the words was changed.

Articles

Cantonese has no equivalent words to the English articles, 'a', 'an' and 'the'. Words meaning 'one' and 'this/that' are used, and often a classifier word, such as *bóon* is required (see the Numbers & Amounts chapter for an explanation of classifers). For example:

I want **a** book.	*ngőh yīu yàt bóon sùe*
	I want **one** classifier book
I want **the** book.	*ngőh yīu nì/góh bóon sùe*
	I want **this/that** classifier book

Nouns

Nouns have no gender or numerical values. Usually they exist as a single character, though they can also exist as a pair or more characters. A single character noun, made up of two words, is the most common.

Adjectives

Adjectives in Cantonese are normally placed in front of the noun, with some exceptions. Sometimes the possessive word *gē* may be placed between the adjective and the noun, however the meaning doesn't change.

good	*hó*
good book	*hó sùe* or *hó gē sùe*

Comparisons

good	*hó*
better	*hó dì*
best	*jūi hó*
cheap	*peng*
cheaper	*peng dì*
the cheapest	*jūi peng*

Pronouns

I/me	*ngőh*	we/us	*ngőh dēi*
you	*nēi*	you (plural)	*nēi dēi*
he/she/ him/her	*kúi*	they/them	*kúi dēi*
this	*nì gőh*	that	*góh gőh*
these	*nì dì*	those	*góh dì*

Verbs

The usage of verbs in Cantonese isn't nearly as complicated and confusing as English verbs can be. The verb stays the same no matter what the tense is, that is, it doesn't change with past, present and future meanings. It also stays the same regardless of the pronoun used.

Here are some typical Cantonese verbs. Some are seldom used in other Chinese dialects.

to carry	*nìng*	擰
to do	*jŏ*	做
to eat	*sīk*	食
to give	*bēi*	俾
to hold	*jà*	揸
to look for	*wán*	揾
to see	*tái*	睇
to sleep	*fān*	瞓
to speak	*góng*	講
to take	*lóh*	攞

To Be

The verb, to be, is simply *hǎi*. It's normally used when two nouns are linked together.

I am American. *ngŏh hǎi měi gwōk yan*
  I *hǎi* America person

To Have

The words *yǎu* and *mŏ* denote 'have' and 'not have' respectively. They are placed in front of the object.

I have a pen. *ngŏh yǎu bàt*
I don't have a car. *ngŏh mŏ chè*

Tense

Tense is not indicated by the verb as it is in English. Additional words such as yesterday, tomorrow, last year, etc are needed to indicate time/tense.

I drink tea.	*ngőh yàm cha*
I drank tea (just now).	*(tau sìn) ngőh yám cha*

- The word *jóh*, placed straight after a verb, indicates that the action is completed:

I have drunk tea.	*ngőh yám jóh cha*
	I drink *jóh* tea
I went.	*ngőh hūi jóh*
	I go *jóh*

- The word *wóoi*, placed immediately in front of the verb, denotes intention as expressed in English by the words 'am going to' or 'will'.

I will go.	*ngőh wóoi hūi*
	I *wóoi* go

- Placed after a verb, the word *gán* means that the action of the verb is being carried out.

I'm going.	*ngőh hūi gán*
	I go *gán*

Commands

In a positive command, you simply have to emphasise the verb:

Go!	*hūi!*
Sit!	*chóh!*
Come here!	*lei!*

- You can also add *chéng*, which means 'please', in front of the verb to make it a more polite and gentle command.

  | Please sit down. | *chéng chóh* |
  | Please come in. | *chéng yăp lei* |

- For a negative command, you have to add *m jún*, meaning 'not allow to', in front of the verb.

  | Don't go! | *m jún hūi* |
  | Don't sit! | *m jún chóh* |

- Sometimes, instead of *m jún*, you will often hear the colloquial word *mǎi:* it means 'don't'.

  | Don't move! | *mǎi yùk* |

Negatives

Simply put *m* in front of the verb or adjective to make them negative.

| (I'm) not buying. | *(ngőh) m mǎai* |
| not pretty | *m lēng* |

Yes & No

'Yes' is indicated by the word *hǎi*; 'no' (not + yes) is *m hǎi*.

Sometimes you can use *hó* which means, 'okay', 'yes' or 'good', and *m hó* meaning the opposite. The word *ngàam* means 'correct' or 'right', while *m ngàam* means 'incorrect' or 'wrong'.

Questions

There are basically three types of questions in Cantonese.

- The first type is a positive/negative or a yes/no question; they can be used with verbs or adjectives. The word *ā* is usually found at the end of the questions. For example:

Are you going (or not)?	*néī hūi m hūi ā?*
	you go not go *ā?*
Are you buying (or not)?	*néī mǎai m mǎai ā?*
	you buy not buy *ā?*
Are you a student (or not)?	*néī hǎi m hǎi hǒk sàng ā?*
	you be not be student *ā?*
Is it pretty (or not)?	*lēng m lēng ā?*
	pretty not pretty *ā?*

- The second type concerns what are known in English as 'question words': 'what', 'when', 'why' etc. These questions need specific answers. They are formed by simply adding the question word to the front of the sentence or the end. For beginners, the simplest way is to say the topic, then add the question word at the end:

Where is the library?	*to sùe gwóon! bìn dǒ ā?*
	library! where?
or	*bìn dǒ hǎi to sùe gwóon ā?*
	where *hǎi* library *ā?*

How?	*dím yéung?*	點樣?
What?	*màt yě?*	乜嘢?
When?	*géi sì?*	幾時?
Where?	*bìn dǒ?*	邊度?
Who?	*bìn gōh?*	邊個?
Why?	*dím gáai?*	點解?

- The third type are the questions with the word *mā*. In English, the position of the verb and subject is often swapped to make a question: 'She is going' becomes 'Is she going?' For these types of questions in Cantonese, you only have to add the word *mā* after your sentence to make it a question.

He/She is a student.	*kúi hǎi hǒk sàng*
Is he/she a student?	*kúi hǎi hǒk sàng mā?*

Possession

To indicate possession, the word *gē* is put after the noun and before the object.

my book	*ngǒh gē sùe*
mine	*ngǒh gē*
yours	*néi gē*

Modals
Obligation

Obligation or duty is indicated by the verb, *yīu*, which is similar to the English 'have to' or 'must'.

You have to pay.	*néi yīu béi chín*

Want & Need

A want or a need is expressed by the word *yīu*.

I want.	*ngǒh yīu*
I don't want.	*ngǒh m yīu*
I want to go.	*ngǒh yīu hūi*
I want to go to yum cha.	*ngǒh yīu hūi yám cha*

A wish or hope is expressed by *séung* or *hèi mong* respectively.

Can

The word 'can' is expressed by the words *hóh yí*. It is placed in front of the verb to indicate the ability to do something.

I can sing.   *ngőh hóh yí chēung*

Classifiers

When you talk about quantities of any noun in Cantonese you need to use a classifier, or 'measure word' as they're better described. The measure word goes between the number and the noun, and there are many words which are used, depending on the noun. Refer to the Numbers & Amounts chapter, section on Measure Words, for more information.

Some Useful Words

after	*jì hău*	之後
also	*dò*	都
and	*tung maai*	同埋
at	*hái*	喺
because	*yàn wāi*	因爲
before	*jì chìn*	之前
but	*bàt gwōh*	不過
if	*yue gwóh*	如果
from ...	*yau ...*	由...
just now	*tau sìn* or *jĭng wā*	頭先,正話
now	*yi gà*	而家
or	*dĭng hái*	定係
to ...	*dō ...*	到
with	*lin maai*	連埋
without	*m lin maai*	唔連埋

Greetings & Civilities

Even if you don't read the rest of this chapter, it's important to memorise these five basic 'magic words'. They are:

(I wish) you well. *nèi hó* 你好
This is similar to 'How are you?' in English.

Please.	*chéng*	請
Thank you.	*dòh jĕ*	多謝
Excuse me.	*m gòi*	唔該
Sorry.	*dūi m jŭe*	對唔住

Greetings

The all-purpose phrases in Cantonese are '(I wish) you well', *nèi hó* and 'good morning', *jó san*, which obviously can only be used in the morning. These two phrases will always come in handy and are worth memorising.

Between friends, you may ask each other, literally 'have you eaten?' and 'have you yum cha-ed?', which aren't expressions of curiosity, but are forms of greeting for the Cantonese people.

How are you? or Are you well?	*nèi hó mā?*	你好嗎?
I wish you well.	*nèi hó*	你好
Good morning.	*jó san*	早晨
Have you eaten?	*sĩk jóh fãan mĕi ā?*	食咗飯未呀?
Have you yum cha-ed?	*yám jóh cha mĕi ā?*	飲咗茶未呀?

22

Although 'good afternoon' and 'good evening' do exist, these terms are rarely used nowadays, except maybe for formal occasions.

| Good afternoon. | *ng̃ ngòn* | 午安 |
| Good evening. | *mǎan ngòn* | 晚安 |

Here are some more useful greetings that could be used to greet someone you know or someone you have met before.

What are you doing?	*néî jõ gán màt yẽ ā?*	你做緊乜嘢呀?
How are (you) recently?	*gãn lói dím ā?*	近來點呀?
Where are you going?	*néî hūi bìn dõ ā?*	你去邊度呀?

Replies

Reply to 'good morning', *jó san*, with the same, *jó san*. Some useful replies include:

I am fine.	*ngõh géi hó*	我幾好
Fine.	*géi hó*	幾好
Fine, and you?	*géi hó, néî nè?*	幾好，你呢?
Not bad.	*m chōh*	唔錯
So so.	*ma má*	麻麻

In reply to 'where are you going?', *néî hūi bìn dõ ā?*:

I'm going ...	*ngõh hūi ...*	我去...
to the office	*fàan gùng*	番工
to school	*fàan hõk*	番學
to yum cha	*yám cha*	飲茶

Goodbyes

The easiest way is to say 'goodbye' or 'bye' in English. The most common phrase *bàai bāai* has been adopted from the English.

Bye.
    bàai bāai   拜拜

Come again please.
    dàk haan chèng jōi lei   得閒請再嚟

See you!
    jōi wŏoi!   再會

See you! (colloquial)
    jōi gīn!   再見

See you another time.
    dǎi yĭ si gīn   第二時見

See you soon.
    chi dì jōi gīn   遲啲再見

See you tomorrow.
    tìng yăt jōi gīn   聽日再見

Bon voyage.
    yàt faan fùng sūn   一帆風順

Have a safe trip.
    yàt lŏ ping ngòn   一路平安

Civilities

Conversation isn't very straightforward in Cantonese. If you are talking over dinner, for instance, sometimes you may chat until dessert before you get to the real topic/request/intention. It's the same when doing business; Chinese businesspeople are more subtle in their approach than Westerners, and like to exchange small talk before getting serious.

Attracting Someone's Attention

Being a foreigner in Guangdong and Guangxi is attention-seeking enough, so you don't have to worry about not being able to draw someone's attention. In fact you may have to put up with a great deal of staring and pointing. However, in the unlikely scenario that you can't draw attention to yourself, shout something, anything. Maybe people won't understand what you're saying, but the *fact* that you're shouting is enough to grab their attention.

In the case of an emergency, refer to the Emergencies chapter.

Come quickly!
    fāai dì gwōh lei!   快啲過嚟
Come here quickly and have a look
    at this.
    néî děi fāai dì gwōh lei tái   你哋快啲過嚟睇

Drawing a particular person's attention:

Excuse me...
    dūi m jǔe, ... or   對唔住, . . .
    m gòi, ...   唔該, . . .
Can you please ...?
    m gòi, chéng...   唔該, 請 . . .
Excuse me, come here please.
    m gòi, chéng gwōh lei nì dǒ 唔該, 請過嚟呢度
Please come and help.
    m gòi, chèng gwōh lei bòng sáu 唔該, 請過嚟幫手

The word *wāi* or *wēi* is similar to the English word 'hey', being an informal way of attracting someone's attention. It's not a word that is used regularly between close friends and is not usually associated with politeness or respect, so avoid using it if you can.

Requests & Thanks

The magic word is 'please', *chéng*; when followed by a verb it means 'please, do me a favor and ... '.

Please sit down.	*chéng chóh*	請坐
Please start.	*chéng hòi chí*	請開始
Please wait a while.	*chéng dáng yàt jǎn*	請等一陣

The phrase *chéng mǎn* 'may I ask....?' may be added to most questions, making them more respectful and polite.

Who, may I ask, are you looking for?
  chéng mǎn něi wán bìn yàt wái ā? 請問你搵邊一位呀?
May I ask if Mr. Chan is home?
  *chéng mǎn chan sìn sàang hái m
  hái ngùk kéi ā?* 請問陳先生喺唔喺屋企呀?
Yes, he is here.
  hái, kúi hái dǒ 喺, 佢喺度
No, he isn't here.
  m hái, kúi m hái dǒ 唔喺, 佢唔喺度
May I ask where the toilet is?
  chéng mǎn chī sóh hái bìn dǒ ā? 請問廁所喺邊度呀?

The word 'please', *chéng*, plus a gesture with the hand (towards a door, for example) means 'after you'.

Don't forget the word 'thank you':

| Thank you. (in advance) | *dòh jě sìn or m gòi sìn* | 多謝先 唔該先 |

| Thank you. | *dòh jē* | 多謝 |
| Thank you very much. | *dòh jē sāai* or *m gòi sāai* | 多謝晒 唔該晒 |

Apologies

The English phrase 'I'm sorry' is common enough for most Cantonese people to understand.

Sorry!	*dūi m jūe*	對唔住
Very sorry!	*hó dūi m jūe*	好對唔住
regret	*hó wai hām*	好遺憾
Never mind!	*m gán yīu*	唔緊要

Some Useful Phrases

Thank you for your kindness.
dòh jē néi yáu sàm — 多謝你有心

You don't have to do that.
m sái hāak hēi or — 唔駛客氣
m hó yī sī — 唔好意思

You don't have to say sorry.
m sái dūi m jūe — 唔駛對唔住

You don't have to say thank you.
m sái dòh jē or — 唔駛多謝
m sái m gòi — 唔駛唔該

Forms of Address

More often than not, when asked what their names are, Cantonese people will give you their surnames, whereas Westerners give their first names. After establishing the surname, you should add a title (Mr, Miss, Mrs, etc) that is said after their surnames. The title *always* comes last.

It's best not to address the Cantonese by their first name(s) even if they have told you what they were; only close friends would call each other by their first names. Decades of Western influences have resulted in most young Cantonese people having an English given name, as well as a Chinese name. The given name precedes the surname, eg Sally *Lau* Suk-Ling. In most cases, it's fine to call her Sally. (See also the section on Titles in this chapter.)

Typically, men address each other by their surnames, however, good friends show their 'affections' or informalities by adding the prefix *ā* to the surname, for example, *ā Lau*. This is used to and amongst the younger generation only. Similarly, the prefix *lŏ* is for older males, as in the case of *lŏ Lau*. Remember, these are used only between close friends or people whose relationship is fairly informal.

May I ask your name?
   chéng mán gwāi sīng ā?   請問貴姓呀?
My surname is (Lau).
   síu sīng (lau)   小姓(劉)
How should I address you?
   dím chìng fòo néî ā?   點稱呼你呀?
You may call me (A-Lau)/(Lo-Lau).
   gīu ngŏh (ā láu)/(lŏ láu) dàk lā   叫我(亞劉)/(老劉)得喇

Surnames

There are thousands of surnames. Most are one word, a few are two words; rarely are they more than two words. Here are some examples:

Au-Yeung	*ngàu yeung*	歐陽
Chan	*chan*	陳

Cheung	*jèung*	張
Ho	*hoh*	何
Lau	*lau*	劉
Lee or Li	*léi*	李
Ma	*má*	馬
Tang	*dǎng*	鄧
Tse	*jē*	謝
Wong	*wong*	王/黃
Yeung	*yeung*	楊

Traditionally, a married woman would adopt her husband's surname which would then become a prefix to her maiden (full) name, thus creating her legal name. This may then become a little confusing, as it would now be acceptable to call her by her married surname (Mrs Chan), maiden name (Miss Ma lei-lei), given name or even her legal name (Madam Chan Ma lei-lei).

Titles

In English, we say the title first, then first and second names and the last name; but in Chinese, the order is different. The surname is addressed first, then the first and second names, and lastly, the title. For example, Ms Suk-Ling *Lau* becomes *lau sŭk ling nŭi sī*.

The beauty of this language is that, if you can't remember or if you don't know the surname, addressing someone by their title only – Dr, Teacher, and so on – is fairly acceptable.

Here are some common titles:

Mr ...	... *sìn sàang*	...先生
Miss ...	... *síu jé*	...小姐
Mrs ...	... *tāai táai*	...太太
Madam ...	... *nŭi sī*	...女士
Ms ...	... *nŭi sī*	...女士

The following words may also be applied with or without a surname.

Chairman	... *júe jīk*	...主席
Dr ...	... *bŏk sī*	...博士
Doctor (medical) ...	... *yì sàng*	...醫生
Inspector (police)	... *bòng báan*	...幫板
Manager	... *gìng léi*	...經理

Managing Director	... *dúng sī jéung*	...董事長
Master (skilled tradesperson)	... *sì fóo*	...師傅
President	... *júe jīk*	...主席
Professor ...	... *gāau sāu*	...教授
Supervisor	... *júe yām*	...主任
Teacher	... *ló sì*	...老師

For the younger generation, some relative's terms can be used when meeting people for the first time. The terms are aunty, *ā yì*, and uncle, *sùk sùk*, and *bāak bāak*, which is normally addressed to a female/male who is roughly their parents' age. The word granny, *poh póh*, is used when addressing an elderly woman; *sāi bāak*, an elderly male.

These terms are associated with a certain closeness, or affection. It's best to ask how people wish to be addressed.

Body Language

The Cantonese people have been in contact with and influenced by Western culture for a long time, most notably since the Ming Dynasty. Although generally it's still frowned upon by the more reserved and conservative Cantonese people, it's not surprising to see some signs of affection between people in public, eg holding hands. The younger generation are perhaps the main 'culprits', they are more willing to walk arm in arm with friends of the same sex or otherwise, or even hug in public! Avoid showing too much affection with friends when in public, however, as some people may be offended by it.

Although pointing isn't offensive, it's more polite to point with your hand, with the palm facing up.

To most, shaking hands or nodding is sufficient when meeting people. Some may bow as a sign of respect (of age or rank), the deeper the bow, the deeper the (gesture of) respect.

The best body language is the universal language of smiling.

Teeth

Small Talk

Generally, the Cantonese people are very reserved and conservative, especially when meeting new people. This reserve is doubled when meeting foreigners. Try to make conversation. Throughout this book, you'll find a range of topics and vocabulary that you can use during conversations.

It's best if you don't talk about the more serious or sensitive issues like politics, religion and the Chinese people's private lives, not during the first meeting anyway.

Meeting People

Unlike Westerners who can easily start a conversation with 'Isn't the weather nice today?', or 'How are you?', it's a lot harder starting a conversation with a Cantonese person, especially with the language barrier. The simplest and perhaps the best ice breaker is to ask an easy-to-answer and/or common question that will most probably generate a response. For example you can ask for the time, borrow a lighter if you are a smoker, confirm the correct bus route or even ask if you could have a picture taken. Most Cantonese people are more than willing to help you, although in this last instance may become reluctant if you want a picture *with* them. No matter what happens, smiling helps break the ice.

Refer also to the Greetings & Civilities chapter.

What time is it?
   chéng mǎn yi gà géi dím jùng ā?   請問而家幾點鐘呀？
Can I use your lighter?
   hóh m hóh yǐ jē gōh dá fóh gèi   可唔可以借個打火機
   yǔng ā?   用呀？
Can you lend me a hand?
   hóh m hóh yǐ bòng ngóh sáu ā?   可唔可以幫我手呀？
Can you please take a picture
for me?
   hóh m hóh yǐ bòng ngóh yíng   可唔可以幫我影
   jèung séung ā?   張相呀？
I am going to ..., what about you?
   ngóh yīu hūi ..., néi nè?   我要去...,你呢？
What is this/that?
   nì/góh dì hǎi màt yế lei gā?   呢/嗰啲係乜嘢嚟㗎？

Nationalities

Which country do you come from?
nếi hái bìn gōh gwōk gà lei gā? 你喺邊個國家嚟㗎?
What nationality are you?
nếi hǎi bìn gwōk yan ā? 你係邊國人呀?

To show your nationality, simply add the word 'person', *yan*, after
the name of the country .

I come from (the USA).
ngốh hái (mếi gwōk) lei 我喺(美國)嚟
I am (American).
ngốh hǎi (mếi gwōk) yan 我係(美國)人

America	*mếi gwōk*	美國
Australia	*ngō jàu*	澳洲
Belgium	*béi lẽi si*	比利時
Bangladesh*	*mǎang gà làai*	孟加拉
Cambodia*	*gáan po jǎai*	柬埔寨
Canada	*gà na dǎai*	加拿大
China	*jùng gwōk*	中國
Denmark*	*dàan mǎk*	丹麥
Egypt	*ngài kắp*	埃及
Europe	*ngàu jàu*	歐洲
Finland*	*fàn laan*	芬蘭
France*	*fāat gwōk*	法國
Germany*	*dàk gwōk*	德國
Holland*	*hoh làan*	荷蘭
Hong Kong	*hèung góng*	香港
India*	*yān dỗ*	印度
Indonesia*	*yān nei*	印尼
Ireland	*ngõi yǐ laan*	愛爾蘭

Israel*	*yí sìk līt*	以色列
Italy*	*yī dàai lēi*	意大利
Japan*	*yàt bóon*	日本
Korea*	*hon gwōk*	韓國
Laos*	*liu gwōk*	寮國
Malaysia	*mǎ loi sài ā*	馬來西亞
New Zealand	*náu sài laan*	紐西蘭
Norway*	*noh wài*	挪威
Philippines*	*fèi lūt bàn*	菲律賓
Russia*	*ngoh loh sì*	俄羅斯
Singapore	*sìng gā bòh*	星加坡
Spain*	*sài bàan nga*	西班牙
Sweden*	*sūi dín*	瑞典
Switzerland*	*sūi sī*	瑞士
Thailand*	*tāai gwōk*	泰國
UK	*yìng gwōk*	英國
USA	*méi gwōk*	美國
Vietnam*	*yūet naam*	越南

Are you (Vietnamese)?
  nèi hǎi m hǎi (yūet naam) yan ā?   你係唔係(越南)人呀?
I am not (Vietnamese), I am
  (Indonesian).
    ngőh m hǎi (yūet naam) yan, ngőh   我唔係(越南)人,我
      hǎi (yān nei) yan   係(印尼)人

You may also add the word 'language', *wá*, to some countries
(indicated above with an asterisk).

I speak (Spanish) and (Italian).
  ngőh sìk góng (sài bàan nga wá)   我識講(西班牙話)
    tung maai (yī dàai lēi wá)   同埋(意大利話)

The words *fàan gwái* and *gwái ló* literally mean 'foreign devils' and are often used in Hong Kong. It used to have a negative connotation but nowadays people use it as a substitution for the word Westerners without second thought. There were even groups of Westerners participating in the Dragon Boat races in Hong Kong who named themselves *fàan gwái* and *gwái ló*.

Age

Refer to the Numbers & Amounts chapter for your particular age.

How old are you?
    chéng mǎn néî géi dòh sūi ā?   請問你幾多歲呀？

The above is the most common question when asking someone's age. The following would be better when asking the age of elderly people.

    chéng mǎn gwāi gàng ā?   請問貴庚呀？
    chéng mǎn néî géi dǎai nin géi lā?   請問你幾大年紀囉？

When asking children, you may use:
    géi dòh sūi lā?   幾多歲囉？

Most Chinese people like you to guess their ages. Normally, the elderly would be happy if your guess was younger than their real ages. The opposite happens with teenagers or young adults.

Guess how old I am.
    néî góo hǎ ngóh géi dòh sūi?   你估吓我幾多歲？
I think you are (25) years old.
    ngóh góo néî gàm nin (yǐ sǎp nǧ)   我估你今年(25)歲
    sūi

Zodiac

Unlike the Western zodiac, where 12 signs exist within each year and your sign is determined by the day and month you were born, the Chinese zodiac is separated into yearly signs, each based on animals, and your sign depends on the year you were born. The first zodiac sign is the rat, the second the ox, and so on. The Chinese base their zodiac on the lunar calendar, so each sign recurs every 12th year. 1984 was the Year of the Rat, so in another twelve years, in 1996, it will also be the Year of the Rat. 1985 was the Year of Ox, as will be 1997, and 2009.

Very often, instead of asking people how old they are, Chinese people might ask what Year (of the zodiac) a person belongs to, and subsequently they can work out the age. Traditionally, a minority of Cantonese people believe that some zodiac signs don't match. For example, a person born in the Year of the Tiger (being a member of the Cat family) and a person born in the Year of the Rat shouldn't get married.

rat	*súe*	鼠
ox	*ngau*	牛
tiger	*fóo*	虎
rabbit	*tō*	兔
dragon	*lung*	龍
snake	*se*	蛇
horse	*mǎ*	馬
sheep	*yeung*	羊
monkey	*hau*	猴
rooster	*gài*	雞
dog	*gáu*	狗
pig	*jùe*	豬

What Year (of the zodiac) were you born in?

nĕi hái màt yĕ nin chùt sāi gā? 你喺乜嘢年出世㗎?

Which zodiac do you belong to?

nĕi hãi sũk yùe bìn yàt gōh sàng chīu ā? 你係屬於邊一個生肖呀?

I was born in the Year of the (Pig).

ngõh hãi (jùe) nin chùt sāi gē 我係(豬)年出世嘅

I belong to the Year of the (Dragon).

ngõh hãi sũk (lung) gē 我係屬(龍)嘅

Occupations

What is your occupation?

nĕi gē jìk yĭp hãi màt yĕ ā? 你嘅職業係乜嘢呀?

This may be the most direct question when asking one's occupation. There are other ways; *jõ sĭng hong ā?* or *jõ bìn yàt hong ā?* literally meaning, 'Which honourable business do you belong to?'; *hái bìn dŏ fāat choi ā?* literally meaning, 'From where do you make your money?' (Where do you work?)

I am a/an ...	*ngõh hãi...*	我係...
accountant	*wõoi gāi*	會計
actor	*yín yuen*	演員
architect	*gīn jõk sì*	建築師
athlete	*wãn dũng yuen*	運動員
businessperson	*sèung yan*	商人
chef	*chue sì*	廚人
chemist	*yĕuk jài sì*	藥劑師
clerk	*man yuen*	文員
doctor	*yì sàng*	醫生
driver	*sì gèi*	司機

engineer	*gùng ching sì*	工程師
farmer	*nung fòo*	農夫
fisher	*yue fòo*	漁夫
hawker	*síu fáan*	小販
homemaker	*júe fốo*	主婦
interpreter	*fàan yĭk*	翻譯
journalist	*gēi jé*	記者
labourer	*gùng yan*	工人
lawyer	*lũt sì*	律師
manager	*gìng léī*	經理
musician	*yàm ngõk gà*	音樂家
nurse	*wõo sĩ*	護士
office worker	*jìk yuen*	職員
pastor/priest	*mũk sì*	牧師
photographer	*sĩp yíng sì*	攝影師
poet	*sì yan*	詩人
politician	*jĭng jĭ gà*	政治家
professor	*gāau sǎu*	教授
public servant	*gùng mõ yuen*	公務員
receptionist	*jĭp dõi yuen*	接待員
salesperson	*sǎu fõh yuen*	售貨員
sales representative	*ying yĭp dõi bíu*	營業代表
scientist	*fòh hõk gà*	科學家
soldier	*gwàn yan*	軍人
student	*hõk sàang*	學生
teacher	*gāau sì*	教師
technician	*gēi gùng*	技工
tourist	*yau hāak*	遊客
waiter	*fóh gēi*	伙記
writer	*jõk gà*	作家

policeman (in China)
gùng ngòn
公安
policeman (in Hong Kong)
gíng chāat
警察

Some Useful Words & Phrases

amateur	*yĩp yue*	業餘
full-time job	*chuen jìk*	全職
looking for a job	*wán gán gùng*	搵緊工
profession	*jùen yĩp*	專業
retired	*tūi yàu*	退休

side job	*gìm jìk*	兼職
specialist	*jùen gà*	專家
unemployed (in China)	*dõi yĩp*	待業
unemployed (in Hong Kong)	*sàt yĩp*	失業

Religion

What is your religion?

néî sūn màt yế gāau gā? 你信乜嘢教㗎?

I am (a) ...	*ngốh sūn ...*	我信...
Buddhist	*fãt gāau*	佛教
Catholic	*tìn júe gāau*	天主教
Christian	*gèi dùk gāau*	基督教
Confucian	*húng gāau*	孔教
Hindu	*yān dõ gāau*	印度教
Jewish	*yau tāai gāau*	猶太教
Muslim	*yì sì laan gāau* or	伊斯蘭教
	wooi gāau	回教
Protestant	*sàn gāau*	新教
Taoist	*dõ gāau*	道教

I am not religious.

ngốh m sūn gāau 我唔信教

Do you go to church/mass?

yấu mố hūi (lấi bāai tong)/ 有冇去(禮拜堂)/
(mõng nei sāat) ā? (望彌撒)呀?

Some Useful Words

ancestor worship	*bāai jó sìn*	拜祖先
Buddhist temple	*fāt jí*	佛寺
cathedral	*dāai gāau tóng*	大教堂
Catholic church	*sīng tóng*	聖堂
church	*lǎi bāai tong*	禮拜堂
Confucian temple	*húng mǐu*	孔廟
Dhyana temple	*sim yúen*	禪院
god	*san*	神
monastery	*sàu dǒ yúen*	修道院
mosque	*chìng jàn jí*	清眞寺
pagoda	*tāap*	塔
shrine	*chi tóng*	祠堂
Taoist temple	*dǒ gwōon* or	道觀
	gùng	宮
temple	*míu* or *jí*	廟/寺
worship god	*bāai san*	拜神

Family

Are you married?
　néi gīt jóh fàn měi ā?　　你結咗婚未呀?
I am married.
　ngǒh gīt jóh fàn　　我結咗婚
I am single.
　ngǒh jūng hǎi dàan sàn　　我重係單身
How many children do you have?
　néi yǎu géi dòh gōh jái nǚi ā?　　你有幾多個仔女呀?
I don't have any children.
　ngǒh jūng měi yǎu jái nǚi　　我重未有仔女

I have ... (and ...).	*ngőh yáu ...*	我有...
	(tung maai ...)	(同埋...)
a son	*yàt gōh jái*	一個仔
two sons	*léung gōh jái*	兩個仔
a daughter	*yàt gōh nűi*	一個女
three daughters	*sàam gōh nűi*	三個女

Do you have a boy/girlfriend?

nếi yáu mő(naam)/(nűi) pang yáu ā? 你有冇(男)/(女)朋友呀?

Yes. (I have)

yáu 有

No. (I don't have)

mő 冇

How many (brothers)/(sisters) do you have?

nếi yáu géi dòh (hìng dāi)/ 你有幾多(兄弟)/
(jí mőoi) ā? (姊妹)呀?

I don't have any brothers or sisters.

ngőh mő hìng dāi jí mőoi 我冇兄弟姊妹

I have ... (and ...).	*ngőh yáu ...*	我有...
	(tung maai ...)	(同埋...)
a brother	*yàt gōh hìng dāi*	一個兄弟
a sister	*yàt gōh jí mőoi*	一個姊妹
two brothers	*léung gōh hìng dāi*	兩個兄弟
three sisters	*sàam gōh jí mőoi*	三個姊妹

I am ...	*ngőh hāi ...*	我係...
divorced	*lei jóh fàn*	離咗婚
separated	*fàn jóh gùi*	分咗居
a solo parent	*dăam chàn*	單親
widow	*gwá főo*	寡婦

Family Members

The Chinese use certain words for their own family members and different words for others' family members.

Here are some examples of traditional and formal usage:

This is ...	nì gōh hǎi ...	呢個係...
my father	gà fōo	家父
my husband	ngōi jí	外子
my mother	gà mó	家母
my wife	nōi jí	內子

Is this your ...?	nì wái hǎi m hǎi ... ā?	呢位係唔係...呀?
daughter	lǐng chìn gàm	令千金
elder brother	lǐng hìng	令兄
elder sister	lǐng jí	令姊
father	lǐng jùen	令尊
husband	jùen fòo	尊夫
mother	lǐng tóng	令堂
son	lǐng lóng	令郎
wife	jùen fòo yán	尊夫人
younger brother	lǐng dái	令弟
younger sister	lǐng móoi	令妹

For casual conversation, use the following words:

He/She is my	kúi hǎi ngóh gē ...	佢係我嘅...
aunt	ā yì	阿姨
boyfriend	naam pang yáu	男朋友
child	sāi ló gòh	細路哥
daddy	ba bà	爸爸
daughter	nǔi	女

elder brother	*goh gòh*	哥哥
elder sister	*je jè*	姐姐
eldest brother	*dãai ló*	大佬
father	*fõo chàn*	父親
friend	*pang yáu*	朋友
girlfriend	*nũi pang yáu*	女朋友
grandfather	*jó fõo*	祖父

grandmother	*jó mố*	祖母
husband (colloquial)	*lố gùng*	老公
husband	*jěung fòo*	丈夫
mother	*mố chàn*	母親
mummy	*ma mà*	媽媽
old friend	*ló yấu*	老友
relative	*chàn chìk*	親戚
son	*jái*	仔
uncle	*sùk sùk*	叔叔
wife	*tāai táai*	太太
wife (colloquial)	*lố pốh*	老婆
younger brother	*dai dái*	弟弟
younger brother (colloquial)	*sāi ló*	細佬
younger sister	*mooi móoi*	妹妹
younger sister (colloquial)	*sāi móoi*	細妹

Expressing Feelings

When asking any of the following questions, the adjective is repeated. Thus the query 'are you hungry?', *nếi ngốh m ngốh ā?*, is literally translated as 'you hungry not hungry ā?', meaning 'are you hungry (or not)?'

Are you ...?	*nếi ... m ... ā?*	你...唔...呀?
angry	*nàu*	嬲
ashamed	*cháu*	醜
cold	*dūng*	凍
happy	*hòi sàm*	開心

hot	*yīt*	熱
hungry	*ngōh*	餓
noisy	*cho*	嘈
sad	*sèung sàm*	傷心
scared	*gèng*	驚
sleepy	*ngáan fān*	眼瞓
thirsty	*háu hōt*	口渴
tired	*gwǒoi*	癐
well	*hó*	好
worried	*dàam sàm*	擔心

There is another typical colloquial Cantonese word *dīm* meaning able to do, well done, and success: *kūi hó dīm* means 'he's a/made great success'.

Replies

When answering, add the appropriate adjective from above to the following stems:

I am very ...	*ngőh hó ...*	我好...
I am not very ...	*ngőh m hǎi hó ...*	我唔係好...

Interests & Hobbies

While some Cantonese people will be upfront and tell you how or what they feel, others prefer not to express their opinions. A polite smile and a nod probably means that you have crossed the line and you should stop. On the other hand, you may find it hard to stop some enthusiastic Cantonese people from talking!

What do you like?
néi jùng yī dì màt yế ā?   你中意啲乜嘢呀?

What is your hobby?
néi yẩu màt yế sī hō ā?   你有乜嘢嗜好呀?

Do you like ...?
néi jùng m jùng yī ... ā?   你中唔中意...呀?

I like ... .
ngőh jùng yī ...   我中意...

I don't like ... .
ngőh m jùng yī ...   我唔中意...

animals	*dũng màt*	動物
chess	*jùk kéi*	捉棋
Chinese food	*jùng chàan*	中餐
classical music	*góo dín yàm ngõk*	古典音樂
dancing	*tīu mő*	跳舞
discos	*dìk sī gò*	的士高
driving	*jà chè*	揸車
fishing	*dīu yúe*	釣魚
going shopping	*haang gùng sì*	行公司
Hong Kong	*hèung góng*	香港
Japanese food	*yãt bóon chàan*	日本餐
jogging	*páau bõ*	跑步
karaoke	*kà làai O K*	卡拉 O K
mahjong	*dá ma jēuk*	打麻雀
music	*yàm ngõk*	音樂
popular music	*lau hang yàm ngõk*	流行音樂
reading	*tái sùe*	睇書
sport	*wãn dũng*	運動
swimming	*yau súi*	游水

travelling	*lűi hang*	旅行
watching football	*tái jùk kau*	睇足球
Western food	*sài chàan*	西餐

Language Difficulties

I don't speak Cantonese.
  ngőh m sìk góng gwòng dùng wá   我唔識講廣東話
I don't speak Chinese.
  ngőh m sìk gòng jùng mán   我唔識講中文
Do you speak English?
  néi sìk m sìk góng yìng mán ā?   你識唔識講英文呀?
Do you have an interpreter?
  yáu mő yan fàan yīk ā?   有冇人翻譯呀?
How do you say that in (Cantonese)/
  (English)?
  nì gōh hái (gwóng dùng wá)/   呢個喺(廣東話)/
    (yìng mán) dím góng ā?   (英文)點講呀?
Can you repeat that please?
  chéng jōi góng yàt chī   請再講一次
Could you speak louder/slower please?
  chéng góng (dāai sèng)/(mãan) dì   請講(大聲)/(慢)啲
Please point to the phrase in the book.
  chéng hái sùe dő wán néi góh gūi   請喺書度搵你嗰句
Let me see if I can find it in this book.
  dáng ngőh wán há nì bóon sùe tái   等我搵吓呢本書睇
    há yáu mő   吓有冇?
Do you understand?
  néi ming m ming ā?   你明唔明呀?
I understand.
  ngőh ming   我明

I don't understand.
  ngőh m ming   我唔明
What does it mean?
  màt yé yī sì ā?   乜嘢意思呀?

Tongue

Getting Around

Public transport in Hong Kong is convenient, clean, cheap, very frequent and available from early morning till midnight. If you have a detailed and accurate map of the transport routes, you shouldn't have to ask anyone for directions. Everything normally runs on time. Taxis are abundant so there shouldn't be any troubles getting around in Hong Kong. Being so close to mainland China, Hong Kong ,o offers direct bus/train/ferry services to most of the major cities.

The transport situation in Macau is very similar to that found in Hong Kong. However, there are fewer modes of transport to choose from, and they run less frequently.

Getting around in China can be a little more troublesome and complicated. The main problems are the language barrier (hardly anyone speaks English), there are fewer timetables (if any) available to visitors, and buses, trains and even the domestic airlines aren't very punctual. Times and routes may change without any notice whatsoever and there are occasions when the locals and foreigners are charged differently.

You have to be very careful of pickpockets, especially in Hong Kong and Guangzhou, when visiting crowded markets, travelling in a full bus or walking on busy streets.

I'd like to go to ...
   ngőh séung hūi ...   我想去...
How can I get to ... ?
   ... dím yéung hūi ā?   ...點樣去呀?

Which (bus) do I take to get to ...?
hūi ... yīu chóh bìn yàt gā (bà sí) ā? 去...要坐邊一架 (巴士)呀?

Is there another way to get there?
yáu mố dāi yĭ tiu lố hūi ā? 有冇第二條路去呀?

What time does the next ... leave/arrive?	*hằ yàt bàan ... géi dím jùng hòi/dō ā?*	下一班...幾 點鐘開/到呀?
bus	*bà sí*	巴士
ferry	*suen*	船
train	*fóh chè*	火車
tram	*dĩn chè*	電車
plane	*fèi gèi*	飛機

Finding Your Way

There is a Chinese idiom *lố jõi háu bìn*, literally translated as 'the road is next to your mouth', which means that all you have to do is ask. Don't hesitate to ask for help.

Where is the ...?	*... hái bìn dõ ā?*	...喺邊度呀?
airport	*gèi cheung*	機場
bus stop	*bà sí jăam*	巴士站
bus terminal	*bà sí júng jăam*	巴士總站
car park	*ting chè cheung*	停車場
ferry pier	*síu lun mǎ tau*	小輪碼頭
helipad	*jĭk sìng gèi cheung*	直升機場
light train stop	*hìng tĭt jăam*	輕鐵站
minibus stop	*síu bà jăam*	小巴站

peak tramway station	*lāam chè jăam*	纜車站
pier	*mǎ tau*	碼頭
subway station	*dēi tīt jăam*	地鐵站
taxi stand	*dìk sí jăam*	的士站
ticket office	*sǎu pīu chūe*	售票處
train station	*fóh chè jăam*	火車站
tram stop	*dĭn chè jăam*	電車站

Is it far?	*yűen m yűen ā?*	遠唔遠呀?
Yes, it's far.	*hó yűen*	好遠
Not that far.	*m hăi hó yűen*	唔係好遠
It's quite close.	*hó kán*	好近

Can I walk there?
  haang lŏ hūi m hūi dó gā? 　　行路去唔去到喫?
How far is it to walk?
  haang lŏ yīu géi nŏi ā? 　　行路要幾耐呀?
What is the address?
  chéng mǎn dēi jí hái bìn dŏ ā? 　　請問地址喺邊度呀?
Please write down the address for me.
  m gòi sé gōh dēi jí béi ngőh 　　唔該寫個地址俾我
Could you tell the taxi driver the
  address please?
  m gòi wă gōh dēi jí béi dìk sí sì gèi 　　唔該話個地址俾的士司機
  tèng 　　聽
Please draw a map for me.
  m gòi wăak gōh dēi to béi ngőh 　　唔該畫個地圖俾我
Which direction?
  bìn yàt gōh fòng hēung ā? 　　邊一個方向呀?

Directions

at the corner	*gōk lòk táu*	角落頭
direction	*fòng hēung*	方向
down	*hă bĭn*	卜便
downstairs	*lau hă*	樓下
far away	*yŭen*	遠
inside	*lŭi bĭn*	裡便
left	*jóh bìn*	左便
middle	*jùng gàan*	中間
near	*gān/kān*	近
next to	*gāak lei*	隔離
outside	*ngŏi bĭn*	外便
right	*yău bìn*	右便

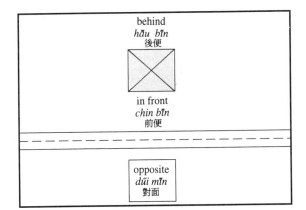

that direction	*góh bìn*	嗰便
this direction	*nì bìn*	呢便
up	*sēung bīn*	上便
upstairs	*lau sēung*	樓上

east	*dùng*	東
north	*bàk*	北
south	*naam*	南
west	*sài*	西

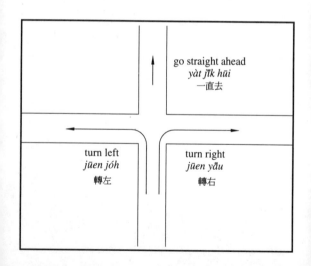

go straight ahead
yàt jīk hūi
一直去

turn left
jūen jóh
轉左

turn right
jūen yáu
轉右

Buying Tickets

When travelling in and out of China, you used to have to buy air, train, long-distance bus and ferry tickets from different outlets. Nowadays, by paying some service charges, you can ask travel agents, service centres or even the reception desk of your hotel to handle the buying for you, which is handy if you're pressed for time. Standby may be another good way to get on board if you can't book a seat.

Most of the public transport in Hong Kong requires the exact fare because no change is given. On buses and trams, you pay when you board by putting the amount in a slot operated by the driver. Everyone pays the fixed amount no matter how far they travel. There are pre-paid tickets, *chúe jīk chè pīu*, available for the subways (MTR) and trains (KCR). They operate on the same principle as the phone cards where an amount is deducted every time the card is used.

Where is the ticket office?
  chéng mǎn sǎu pīu chūe hái bìn dǒ ā?　　請問售票處喺邊度呀?

I would like a (first class) ticket to Guangzhou.
  ngǒh séung mǎai yàt jèung hūi gwóng jàu gē (tau dáng) fèi　　我想買一張去廣州嘅(頭等)飛

How much is it?
  géi dòh chín ā?　　幾多錢呀?

Is there a ticket for the direct bus to Hong Kong today?
  yǎu mǒ gàm yàt hūi hèung góng gē jīk tùng bà sí féi ā?　　有冇今日去香港嘅直通巴士飛呀?

What is the cheapest fare to Hong
   Kong (by ferry)?
   chóh (dāai súen) hūi hèung góng　坐(大船)去香港
   　jūi peng gē fèi yīu géi dòh chín ā?　最平嘅飛要幾多錢呀?
I want to book a ticket for
   (next Wednesday).
   ngőh séung yūe děng　我想預訂
   　(hă sìng kei sàam) gē fèi　(下星期三)嘅飛
I would like to upgrade my ticket.
   ngőh séung bó féi　我想補飛
I want to change to a (soft-seat).
   ngőh séung wōon (yűen jōh)　我想換(軟座)
What is the price difference?
   chà géi dòh chín ā?　差幾多錢呀?
It's full.
   mőon jōh　滿座

adult's ticket	*dāai yan fèi*	大人飛
advance rail ticket office	*fóh chè pīu yūe sāu chűe*	火車票預售處
advance ticket office (general)	*yūe sāu chűe*	預售處
berth	*chong wái*	床位
bottom berth	*hă gāak chong pò*	下格床鋪
middle berth	*jùng gàan chong pò*	中間床鋪
upper berth	*sēung gāal chong pò*	上格床鋪
cabin-class	*dāai chòng wái*	大艙位

cancel	*chúi sìu*	取消
cancelled	*chúi sìu jóh*	取消咗
child's ticket	*síu tung fèi*	小童飛
confirm	*kōk yǐng*	·確認
dormitory bunk	*chong wài*	床位
economy class	*gìng jāi wái*	經濟位
first class	*tau dáng*	頭等
no room	*mǒon jóh*	滿座
no-smoking seat	*gàm yìn wái*	禁煙位
one-way ticket	*dàan chìng fèi*	單程飛
platform ticket (train)	*jǎam toi pīu*	站台票
pre-paid tickets	*chǔe jǐk chè pīu*	儲值車票
refund	*tūi pīu*	退票
return ticket	*loi wooi pīu*	來回票
seat	*jǒh wái*	座位
second class	*yǐ dáng*	二等
student's ticket	*hǒk sàang fèi*	學生飛
ticket office	*sǎu pīu chǔe*	售票處
timetable	*si gàan bíu*	時間表
upgrade ticket	*bó pīu*	補票
window seat	*chèung háu wái*	窗口位

Air

The services at the international airports in China are reasonable, but it's essential to confirm your flights and make sure you know the exact time of departure (times and routes may change without any notice). You also have to be on the lookout for different prices charged to locals and foreigners on domestic flights.

I want to confirm my flight.

ngőh seúng kŏk yĭng ngőh gē   我想確認我嘅班機
bàan gèi

My ticket costs more than his.

ngőh jèung fèi gwāi gwāh kúi góh   我張飛貴過佢嗰張
jèung

This price is higher than normal.

nì gōh gā chin gwāi gwōh ping si   呢個價錢貴過平時

aeroplane	*fèi gèi*	飛機
air bus	*hùng jùng bà sí*	空中巴士
airline ticket	*gèi pīu*	機票
airport	*gèi cheung*	機場
airport tax	*gèi cheung sūi*	機場稅
arrival	*yắp gíng*	入境
boarding	*dàng gèi*	登機
boarding pass	*dàng gèi jĭng*	登機証
business class	*sèung mő hāk wái*	商務客位
customs	*hói gwàan*	海關
customs'	*hói gwàan sàn gō*	海關申報單
declaration	*dàan*	
departure	*chùt gíng*	出境
economy class	*gìng jāi wái*	經濟位

estimated time of arrival	*dō dăat si gāan*	到達時間
estimated time of departure	*héi fèi si gāan*	起飛時間
first class	*tau dáng*	頭等
flight number ... (in China)	*... hŏ hong bàan*	...號航班
flight number ... (in Hong Kong)	*... hŏ bàan gèi*	...號班機
gate	*dàng gèi jăap háu*	登機閘口
gate no ...	*... hŏ jăap háu*	...號閘口
no smoking	*bàt jún kàp yìn*	不准吸煙
non-smoking area	*gām yìn kùi*	禁煙區
passport	*wŏo jĭu*	護照
smoking area	*kàp yìn kùi*	吸煙區
transit	*jūen gèi*	轉機
visa	*chìm jĭng*	簽証
waiting room	*hău gèi sàt*	侯機室

Bus

It's very cheap to travel by local buses in China. You can also travel long distances by bus. The advantage of bus travel includes the chance, during meal breaks, of looking around little towns and villages that you wouldn't normally have the chance to see. The drawbacks are that they are usually crowded and noisy, and the ride is often bumpy and uncomfortable. If unlucky, you may even have to stand for some or even all of the trip.

There are many buses in Hong Kong and they serve different purposes. Some run express while others make frequent stops and are good when you want to see around the city. There are also the more luxurious buses with air-conditioning, but of course they cost more.

Some minibuses are privately owned. Sometimes their fares go up during rush hours, and are even more expensive during storms! To give you an indication, their fares are usually more expensive than buses, but much cheaper than catching a taxi. Some minibuses run 24 hours a day. While the destinations are fixed, the routes and the stops are flexible depending on the traffic and customers' needs.

There are other franchised buses that run express from one destination to another, with fixed prices and routes.

Is this going to the (zoo)?
   nì gā chè hǎi m hǎi hūi   呢架車係唔係去
   (dǒng mǎt yuen) gā?   (動物園)㗎?
I want to get off at ...
   ngǒh séung hái ... lǒk chè   我想喺...落車
Please tell me when we've reached
   that stop.
   chéng néi dō si gīu ngǒh lǒk chè   請你到時叫我落車

air-conditioned bus	*hùng tiu bà sí*	空調巴士
airport bus	*gèi cheung bà sí*	機場巴士
bus (in China)	*gùng gǔng hēi chè*	公共汽車
bus	*bà sí*	巴士
(in Hong Kong)		
bus stop	*bà sí jǎam*	巴士站
bus terminal	*bà sí júng jǎam*	巴士總站
city bus	*sing bà*	城巴
double-decker bus	*sèung chang bà sí*	雙層巴士
feeder bus	*jīp bōk bà sí*	接駁巴士

long-distance bus station	*cheung to hēi chè jăam* or *hāak wăn jăam*	長途汽車站 客運站
minibus (in China)	*mĭn bàau chè*	麵包車
minibus (in Hong Kong)	*síu bà*	小巴
section	*fàn dūen*	分段
shuttle bus	*chùen sòh bà sí*	穿梭巴士
sightseeing bus	*lűi yau bà sí*	旅遊巴士
tunnel bus	*sūi dŏ bà sí*	隧道巴士

Train
Trains & Subways in Hong Kong

How much is the ticket to (Central) by MTR?
chóh dĕi tīt hūi (jùng waan) yīu gēi dòh chín ā?

坐地鐵去(中環)要幾多錢呀?

How many stations before I reach (Shatin)?
nì dŏ hūi (sà tin) yīu dāap géi dòh gōh jăam ā?

呢度去(沙田)要搭幾多個站呀?

At which station should I change over?
hái bìn gōh jăam jūen chè ā?

喺邊個站轉車呀?

Change over at ...
hái ... jūen chè

喺...轉車

| Kowloon-Canton Railway (KCR) | *gáu gwóng tīi lŏ* | 九廣鐵路 |
| Mass Transit Railway (MTR) | *dĕi tīt* | 地鐵 |

Light Rail Transit (LRT)	*hìng tīt*	輕鐵
electric train	*dĭn hēi fā fóh chè*	電氣化火車
subway	*dĕi tīt*	地鐵
subway station	*dĕi tīt jăam*	地鐵站
train station	*fóh chè jăam*	火車站

Major Train & Subway Stations in Hong Kong

Admiralty	*gàm jùng*	金鐘
Causeway Bay	*tung loh waan*	銅鑼灣
Central	*jùng waan*	中環
Chai Wan	*chaai wàan*	柴灣
Kowloon	*gáu lung*	九龍
Kowloon Tong	*gáu lung tong*	九龍塘
Kwun Tong	*gwòon tong*	觀塘
Lo Wu	*loh woo*	羅湖
Mong Kok	*wŏng gōk*	旺角
Quarry Bay	*jàk yue chùng*	鰂魚涌
Shatin	*sà tin*	沙田
Sheung Wan	*sĕung waan*	上環
Tsim Sha Tsui	*jìm sà júi*	尖沙咀
Tsuen Wan	*chuen wàan*	荃灣

Trains in China

Local train tickets are relatively cheap in China, although if you are not travelling first class the journey can be noisy and the carriages crowded and dirty. Some people may even smoke in the non-smoking section of the train.

There are hot water services available on most trains. You can bring your own tea bag, or buy from the 'waiters'. For long-distance travellers, food and drinks are available in the dining car.

Can you help me find my (seat)/(berth) please?

> *chéng bòng ngőh wán ngőh gē (jőh wái)/(chong wái)*   請幫我搵我嘅 （座位)/(床位)

Excuse me, this is my seat.

> *dūi m jŭi, nì gōh hăi ngőh gē wái*   對唔住，呢個係我嘅位

Where is the dining car?

> *chàan chè hái bìn dŏ ā?*   餐車喺邊度呀？

dining car	*chàan chè*	餐車
direct train	*jīk tùng chè*	直通車
express train	*dăk fāai*	特快
fast train	*fāai chè*	快車
first-class waiting room	*yűen jőh hău chè sàt*	軟座侯車室
Guangzhou direct train	*gwóng jàu jīk tùng chè*	廣州直通車
hard-seat (second class)	*ngăang jőh*	硬座
hard-sleeper (second class)	*ngăang ngőh*	硬臥
local train	*pó tùng chè*	普通車
railway station	*fóh chè jāam*	火車站
soft-seat (first class)	*yűen jőh*	軟座
soft-sleeper (first class)	*yűen ngőh*	軟臥
train	*fóh chè*	火車

Taxi

You can hire a taxi anywhere in Hong Kong except on some busy streets where boarding taxis is forbidden at certain times. Taxis run on meters, and the customers will have to pay the levy required for crossing through most of the tunnels. It's important to know that taxis can only serve in their areas. For example, the taxis licensed for the New Territory cannot cross over to the city, but the licence given to the 'city taxis' allows them access throughout Hong Kong. When paying, remember that a tip of about 5% to 10% of the fare is expected.

In China, taxis can be picked up from airport terminals, hotels and even on the streets, but it's best to book a taxi through your hotel if possible. Instead of using a meter, some taxi drivers may want to negotiate a fixed price with you for your journey, or ask you to pay foreign currency instead of Renminbi.

For daily excursions or journeys to more remote areas, where a return trip is needed, it's possible to charter a taxi for half a day or a whole day. In some cases, the driver could also be your guide, but you'll have to ask for an English-speaking or experienced driver when booking.

charter	*bàau chè*	包車
one-day charter	*bàau yàt yăt chè*	包一日車
half-day charter	*bàau bōon yăt chè*	包半日車

I would like to go to ...
  ngőh séung hūi ...   我想去...
How long does it take to go to ...?
  hūi ... yīu géi női ā?   去...要幾耐呀?

I want an English-speaking driver.

ngőh yīu yàt wái sīk góng yìng mán gē sì gèi 我要一位識講英文嘅司機

How much?

géi dòh chín ā? 幾多錢呀?

Thank you.

m gòi sāai 唔該晒

Instructions

Please stop here.

chéng hái nì dõ ting chè 請喺呢度停車

Please stop before the restricted area.

chéng hái gām kùi jì chin ting chè 請喺禁區之前停車

First go to the station, then the airport.

sìn hūi fóh chè jăam, jōi hūi gèi cheung 先去火車站,再去機場

Stop at the next corner.

m gòi hái hă yàt gōh gàai háu ting chè 唔該喺下一個街口停車

Please hurry.

m gói fāai dì 唔該快啲

Please slow down.

m gòi măan dì 唔該慢啲

Please wait here.

chéng hái nì dõ dáng ngőh 請喺呢度等我

I will get off here.

ngőh hái nì dõ lŏk chè 我喺呢度落車

Car

You can only drive in Hong Kong and Macau if you have an international licence. Parking can be a problem in the city areas.

Most tunnels in Hong Kong carry a levy and there are separate lanes for drivers with the exact fare (express lanes) and those needing change.

It's not advisable for visitors to drive in China.

Where can I rent a car?
hái bīn dõ hóh yí jò chè ā?　　　喺邊度可以租車呀?

How much is it for ...?	*jò ... géi dòh chín ā?*	租...幾多錢呀?
one day	*yàt yàt*	一日
three days	*sàam yàt*	三日
one week	*yàt gōh sìng kei*	一個星期

Does that include insurance?
lin m lin bó hím ā?　　　連唔連保險呀?

accident	*yī ngõi*	意外
drivers' licence	*chè paai*	車牌
to get in the car	*séung chè*	上車
to get out of the car	*lõk chè*	落車
insurance	*bó hím*	保險
international driving licence	*gwōk jāi chè paai*	國際車牌
rent a car	*jò chè*	租車

Tunnels in Hong Kong

Aberdeen Tunnel	*hèung góng jái sũi dõ*	香港仔隧道
Airport Tunnel	*gèi cheung sũi dõ*	機場隧道
Cross Harbour Tunnel	*hói dái sũi dõ*	海底隧道

Eastern Harbour Crossing	*dùng kùi hói dái sūi dŏ*	東區海底隧道
Lion Rock Tunnel	*sì jí sàan sūi dŏ*	獅子山隧道
Shing Mun Tunnels	*shing moon sūi dŏ*	城門隧道
Tate's Cairn Tunnel	*dāai lŏ sàan sūi dŏ*	大老山隧道
Tseung Kwan O Tunnel	*jèung gwàn ngò sūi dŏ*	將軍澳隧道

Major Highways in Hong Kong

Island Eastern Corridor	*dùng kùi jáu long*	東區走廊
Tolo Highway	*tō lŏ góng gùng lŏ*	吐露港公路
Tuen Mun Road	*tuen moon gùng lŏ*	屯門公路

Some Useful Words

air	*dá hēi*	打氣
air conditioning	*hùng tiu* or *lăang hēi*	空調/冷氣
battery	*dĭn chi*	電池
brake	*sāat chè jāi*	刹車掣
diesel	*yau jà*	油渣
engine oil	*gái yáu*	偈油
fill up	*yăp yáu*	入油
flat tyre	*bāau tàai*	爆胎
headlight	*chè tau dàng*	車頭燈
highway	*gùng lŏ*	公路
map	*dĕi to*	地圖
parking meter	*ting chè sàu fāi bìu*	停車收費錶
petrol	*hēi yau* or *dĭn yáu*	汽油/電油
radiator	*súi sèung*	水箱
rent a car	*jò chè*	租車

service station	gà yau jăam	加油站
superhighway	chìu kàp gùng lŏ	超級公路
towing a car	tòh chè	拖車
traffic jam	sàt chè	塞車
tyre	chè tàai	車胎
unleaded petrol	bàt ham yuen hēi yau	不含鉛汽油

Boat

China Ferry Terminal	jùng góng sing mǎ tau	中港城碼頭
ferry (cross harbour)	dŏ hói síu lun	渡海小輪
ferry (to China/ Macau)	dăai súen	大船
ferry ticket	suen fèi	船飛
hoverferry	hēi jín suen	氣墊船
hydrofoil	súi yǐk suen	水翼船
jetfoil	pān sě suen	噴射船

junk	*faan suen*	帆船
local village ferry	*gàai dó*	街渡
Macau Ferry Terminal	*góng ngō mǎ tau*	港澳碼頭
Macau Ferry	*ngō móon suen*	澳門船
Star Ferry	*tìn sìng síu lun*	天星小輪
vehicular ferry	*hēi chè dō lun*	汽車渡輪
Yaumati Ferry	*yau ma déi síu lun*	油麻地小輪

Paperwork

address	*dēi jí*	地址
age	*nin ling*	年齡
customs declaration	*hói gwàan sàn gō dàan*	海關申報單
date of birth	*chùt sàng nin yǔet yāt*	出生年月日
itinerary	*hang ching bíu*	行程表
married	*yí fàn*	已婚
name	*sīng ming*	姓名
nationality	*gwōk jīk*	國籍
occupation	*jìk yīp*	職業
passport	*wǒo jīu*	護照
passport number	*wǒo jīu hǒ mǎ*	護照號碼
place of birth	*chùt sàng dēi*	出生地
profession	*jùen yīp*	專業
quarantine	*gím yīk*	檢疫
single	*dàan sàn*	單身
transit	*gwōh gíng*	過境
visa	*chìm jīng*	簽証

Traffic Signs

Most of the traffic signs are similar to those used internationally. But pay attention to different road laws: the most obvious being that in China you drive on the right-hand side of the road, whilst in Hong Kong you drive on the left.

讓	**GIVE WAY**
靠左	**KEEP LEFT**
靠右	**KEEP RIGHT**
不准駛入	**NO ENTRY**
不准停車	**NO PARKING**
不准停車等侯	**NO WAITING**
單程路	**ONE WAY ONLY**
寂靜地帶	**QUIET**
平交道	**RAILWAY CROSSING**
禁區	**RESTRICTED AREA**
慢	**SLOW**
停	**STOP**
斑馬線	**ZEBRA CROSSING**

Other Transport

bicycle	*dàan chè*	單車
boat	*téng jái*	艇仔
funicular railway	*sàan déng lăam chè*	山頂纜車
motorbike	*dīn dàan chè*	電單車

peak tramway	*sàan déng lāam chè*	山頂纜車
pedicab	*sàam lún chè*	三輪車
rent a bicycle	*jò dàan chè*	租單車
rickshaw	*chè jái*	車仔
tramway	*dīn chè*	電車
yacht	*yau téng*	遊艇

Accommodation

The main cities have a wide range of accommodation, ranging from five-star hotels to simple hostels. Most of the luxury hotels have some English-speaking staff, but if you wish to stay in cheap local accommodation, you'll find this chapter will be a great help.

With most accommodation in China, make sure you know the service hours of restaurants and the availability of the hot water supply. Before using high-consumption electrical appliances (such as an iron or heater), consult the reception desk, *fūk mō toi*, first. You should also verify that you are using the correct voltage (220V AC 50Hz) and correct design of the electrical outlets.

The general classification of accommodation is as follows:

Luxury Hotel

hotel	*jáu dīm*	酒店
	fāan dīm	飯店
	bàn gwóon	賓館

Inn, Guesthouse

These have only basic facilities, in the rooms or shared.

inn	*lúi gwóon*	旅館
	lúi sē	旅舍
	hāak jáan	客棧

Apartment, Dormitory

apartment	*gùng yūe*	公寓
dormitory	*sùk sē*	宿舍
guesthouse	*jìu dōi sóh*	招待所
youth hostel	*chìng nin sùk sē*	青年宿舍

Finding Accommodation

If you need assistance in finding accommodation, the information desk in the airport or railway station will help you; or a taxi driver may be a suitable person for you to ask.

Where is a guesthouse?	*bìn dǒ yǎu jìu dǒi sóh ā?*	邊度有招待所呀？
I'm looking for a ... hotel.	*naǒh séung wán yàt gàan ... gē jáu dīm*	我想搵一間... 嘅酒店
cheap	*peng*	平
clean	*gòn jěng*	干淨
good	*hó*	好
near-the-city	*gǎn séng*	近城
near-the-airport	*gǎn gèi cheung*	近機場
nearby	*nì dǒ fǒo gǎn*	呢度附近

At the Hotel
Checking In

Do you have any rooms available?	*yǎu mǒ fóng ā?*	有冇房呀？
Do you have any beds available?	*yǎu mǒ chong wái ā?*	有冇床位呀？
I would like a ...	*ngǒh séung yīu ...*	我想要...
single room	*yàt gàan dàan yan fóng*	一間單人房
quiet room	*yàt gàan chìng jīng gē fóng*	一間清靜嘅房
twin room	*yàt gàan sèung yan fóng*	一間雙人房

big room	*yàt gàan dāai fóng*	一間大房
bed	*yàt gōh chong wái*	一個床位
double bed	*yàt jèung sèung yan chong*	一張雙人床
room in a non-smoking floor	*yàt gōh hái m sīk yìn góh chang gē fóng*	一個喺唔食煙嗰層嘅房

Requirements

I want a room with (a) ...	*ngőh yīu yàt gàan yőu ... gē fóng*	我要一間有...嘅房
harbour view	*hói gíng*	海景
microwave	*mei bòh lo*	微波爐
telephone	*dīn wá*	電話

See Some Useful Words at the end of this chapter for more vocabulary.

Negotiation

How much is it per night?
géi dòh chín yàt máan ā?　幾多錢一晚呀？

How much is it per person?
géi dòh chín yàt gōh yan ā?　幾多錢一個人呀？

Is there a discount for (children)/
(students)?
(sāi lő gòh)/(hők sàang) yőu mő jīt kāu ā?　(細路哥)/(學生)有有折扣呀？

Would I get a discount if I stayed longer?
jūe női dì yőu mő jīt kāu ā?　住耐啲有有折扣呀？

Does it include breakfast?
    lin m lin jó chàan ā?   連唔連早餐呀?

Are there any cheaper ones?
    yǎu mǒ peng dì gē?   有冇平啲嘅?

Can I see the room first?
    hóh m hóh yǐ sìn tái gàan fóng?   可唔可以先睇間房?

Are there any others?
    jūng yǎu mǒ kei tà gē?   重有冇其他嘅?

I like (this)/(that) room.
    ngǒh jùng yī (ni)/(góh) gàan fóng   我中意(呢)/(嗰)間房

It's fine, I'll take this room.
    hó, ngǒh yīu ni gàan fóng   好,我要呢間房

I'm going to stay for ...	*ngǒh dá sūen jǔe ...*	我打算住...
a night	*yàt mǎan*	一晚
two nights	*léung mǎan*	兩晚
a few days	*géi yàt*	幾日
a week	*yàt gōh sìng kei*	一個星期

Service

Where is the ... ?	*chìng mǎn ... hái bìn dǒ ā?*	請問...喺邊度呀?
business centre	*sèung mǒ jùng sàm*	商務中心
conference room	*wǒoi yí sàt*	會議室
dining room	*fǎan tèng*	飯廳
gym	*gīn sàn sàt*	健身室
laundry	*sái sàam fong*	洗衫房
lounge	*yàu sik sàt*	休息室
visitors' lounge	*wǒoi hāak sàt*	會客室

Can I have the key please?
m gòi béi tiu sóh si ngőh　　唔該俾條鎖匙我

Is hot water available all day?
hăi m hăi seng yăt yău yĭt súi ā?　　係唔係成日有熱水呀?

Please wake me up at (6.30 am) tomorrow morning.
m gòi tìng jìu (lŭk dím bōon) gīu séng ngőh　　唔該聽朝(六點半)叫醒我

Please take all my luggage to room (123).
m gòi bòog ngőh bòon dì hang léi hūi (yàt yĭ sàam) hő fòng　　唔該幫我搬啲行李去(123)號房

Please fill up the flask with boiling water.
m gòi gà mőon gōh nűen súi wóo　　唔該加滿個暖水壺

I need (some hangers).
ngőh séung yīu (géi gōh yì gá)　　我想要(幾個衣架)

Please call a taxi for me.
m gòi bòng ngőh gīu gā dìk sí　　唔該幫我叫架的士

Any (bikes) for rent?
yău mő (dàan chè) chùt jò ā?　　有冇(單車)出租呀?

Any ... for me?	*yău mő ngőh gē ... ā?*	有冇我嘅...呀?
fax messages	*chuen jàn*	傳眞
letters	*sūn*	信
telephone messages	*dĭn wá*	電話

I'll be back in (a half)/(one) hour.
ngőh (bōon)/(yàt) gōh jùng tau háu fàan　　我(半)/(一)個鐘頭後番

No visitors.
jě jūet tāam fóng　　謝絕探訪

Please do not disturb.
chìng mắt sò yĩu　　請勿騷擾

Please keep this in the safety box.
nì dì yế chéng sàu hái bó hím sèung bó gwóon　　呢啲嘢請收喺保險箱保管

Do you have a ...?	*yắu mố ... ā?*	有冇...呀?
computer	*dĩn nố*	電腦
copy machine	*yíng yān gèi*	影印機
fax machine	*chuen jàn gèi*	傳眞機
stationery	*man gŭi*	文具
telex	*dĩn chuen*	電傳
typewriter	*dá jĩ gèi*	打字機

Laundry

Could I have these clothes ... please?	*m gòi bòng ngőh ... nì dì sàam*	唔該幫我...呢啲衫
dry-cleaned	*gòn sái*	干洗
ironed	*tōng hó*	熨好
washed	*sái gòn jẽng*	洗干淨

I need it ...	*ngőh ... yīu*	我...要
this afternoon	*gàm yắt ngāan jāu*	今日晏晝
tonight	*gàm mắan*	今晚
tomorrow	*tìng yắt*	聽日

Is my laundry ready?
   ngőh dì sàam sái hó jóh
   měi ā?

我啲衫洗好咗
未呀?

There's a piece missing.
   síu jóh yàt gīn

少咗一件

Requests & Complaints

The room needs to be cleaned.
   chéng dá sō fong gàan

請打掃房間

Please change the (sheets)/(pillow case).
   chéng wőon (chong dàan)/
   (jám tau tō)

請換(床單)/
(枕頭套)

There is no (hot)/(boiling) water.
   mő (yīt)/(gwán) súi

冇(熱)/(滾)水

I don't like this room.
   ngőh m jùng yī nì gàan fóng

我唔中意呢間房

Could I have a different room?
   chéng wőon dầi yī gàan fóng
   béi ngőh

請換第二間房
俾我

It's too	*tāai ...*	太…
big	*dầai*	大
cold	*dūng*	凍
dark	*ngām*	暗
dirty	*wòo jò*	烏糟
hot	*yīt*	熱
noisy	*cho*	嘈
small	*sāi*	細

The ... doesn't work.	... *wăai jóh*	...壞咗
I can't (open)/ (close) the ...	*ngőh (hòi)/(sàan) m dó ...*	我(開)/(閂) 唔到...
I can't turn the ... on.	*ngőh hòi m dó ...*	我開唔到...

See Some Useful Words at the end of this chapter for vocabulary.

It smells.
  yău gwāai mĕi   有怪味
The (toilet)/(sink) is blocked.
  (chi sóh)/(sái sáu poon)   (廁所)/(洗手盆)
  sàk jóh   塞咗
The door is locked.
  fóng moon sóh jóh   房門鎖咗
Can I have the key please?
  m gòi béi sóh si ngőh   唔該俾鎖匙我
My room number is (123).
  ngőh gàan fóng hăi   我間房係
  (yàt yí sàam) hŏ   (123)號
Please have it fixed as soon
  as possible.
  chéng jŭn fāai sàu lĕi   請儘快修理

Checking out

I would like to check out ...	*ngőh ... tūi fóng*	我...退房
now	*yi gà*	而家
tomorrow	*tìng yàt*	聽日
in a while	*dáng yàt jăn*	等一陣

I would like to pay the bill.
  ngőh yi gà béi chín jàau sō   我而家俾錢找數
Can I leave my luggage here for a few
days?
  hóh m hóh yí bòng ngőh bó gwóon   可唔可以幫我保管
  géi yăt ngőh dì hang lēi   幾日我啲行李

I'm returning ... .   *ngőh ... fàan*   我...番
    tomorrow   *tìng yăt*   聽日
    2-3 days   *léung sàam yăt*   兩三日
    next week   *hă gōh sìng kei*   下個星期

Thank you for your hospitality.
  dòh jĕ néi dĕi gē fŭk mŏ   多謝你哋嘅服務

Some Useful Words

address	*dĕi jí*	地址
air-con	*hùng tiu*	空調
babysitter	*lam si bó mŏ*	臨時保姆
baggage	*hang lēi*	行李
balcony	*lŏ toi*	露台
basin	*sái mĭn poon*	洗面盆
bathroom	*chùng léung fóng*	沖涼房
bed	*chong*	床
bill	*jĕung dàan*	賬單
blanket	*mo jìn*	毛氈
bucket	*túng*	桶
check in	*hòi fóng*	開房
check out	*tūi fóng*	退房
cooler	*lăng hēi gèi*	冷氣機

cot	*yūk yìng chong*	育嬰床
cupboard	*bòoi gwāi*	杯櫃
curtain	*chèung lím*	窗簾
door	*fóng moon*	房門
duty manager	*jīk bàan gìng léī*	值班經理
electricity	*dīn*	電
English newspaper	*yìng mán bō jí*	英文報紙
excluded	*mŏ lin maai*	冇連埋
fan	*sīn*	扇
hangers	*yì gá*	衣架
heating	*nŭen hēi*	暖氣
hot water	*yīt súi*	熱水
included	*lin maai*	連埋
iron	*tōng dáu*	熨斗
key	*sóh si*	鎖匙
laundry	*sái sàam fong*	洗衫房
lift (elevator)	*sìng gōng gèi*	昇降機
light bulb	*dàng dáam*	燈胆
lobby	*dāai tong*	大堂
lock	*sóh*	鎖
luggage	*hang léī*	行李
mirror	*gēng*	鏡
mosquito net	*màn jēung*	蚊帳
pillow	*jám tau*	枕頭
pillowcase	*jám tau tō*	枕頭套
porter	*moon fóng*	門房
quiet	*chìng jīng*	清靜
reception desk	*fūk mŏ toi*	服務台
refrigerator	*sūet gwāi*	雪櫃
registration card	*jūe hàak dàng gēi kàat*	住客登記卡

room	*hāak fóng*	客房
room service	*hāak fóng fūk mő*	客房服務
sauna	*sòng na yūk*	桑拿浴
service charge	*fūk mő fāi*	服務費
sheet	*jí*	紙
shower	*fà sá*	花酒
sleeping bag	*sūi dói*	睡袋
soap	*fàan gáan*	番梘
suitcase	*hang léi sèung* or	行李箱
	pei gìp	皮唥
swimming pool	*yau wíng chi*	游泳池
telephone	*dīn wá*	電話
toilet	*chī sóh*	廁所
toilet paper	*chī jí*	廁紙
towel	*mo gàn*	毛巾
TV	*dīn sī*	電視
valuables	*gwāi jūng māt bán*	貴重物品
visitor	*yan hāak*	人客
wardrobe	*yì gwāi*	衣櫃
window	*chèung*	窗

Wine

Around Town

Hong Kong is a city that harmoniously blends modern life with its fair share of culture and tradition. No matter what time of the day it is, you are sure to find something to do and see in this great city. In fact, most of the cities in the Cantonese-speaking regions offer endless activities and 24-hour services.

At the Bank

The banks in Hong Kong are well known for their service, efficiency and the variety of tasks which they can perform. Besides the import and export banking businesses, foreign currency exchange is another major function. After business hours, money exchange shops and the service desk of the hotels can also exchange money, but they may charge higher rates than the banks' official rates.

Credit cards are quite popular and convenient, and travellers' cheques may get an even better rate of exchange than cash.

In Macau, currency rates are worth marginally less than the Hong Kong dollar. However, Hong Kong dollars are often more welcome than Macau dollars, so if you're coming from or going on to Hong Kong, skip the Macau money. Likewise in some areas of southern China, Hong Kong and other foreign currencies are often more welcome than the local Renminbi.

account	*wõo háu*	戶口
airwaybill	*hùng wǎn tai dàan*	空運提單
amount	*ngan mǎ*	銀碼
bank	*ngan hong*	銀行
bankdraft	*ngan hong bóon pīu*	銀行本票

85

bank manager	*ngan hong gìng léi*	銀行經理
banknote	*jí bǎi*	紙幣
black market	*hàk sí*	黑市
buying rate	*mǎai yǎp gā*	買入價
cash	*yǐn gàm*	現金
cashier	*chùt nǎap*	出納
cheque	*jì pīu*	支票
coins	*sūi ngán*	碎銀
counter	*gwǎi tói*	櫃台
credit card	*sūn yŭng kàat*	信用卡
deposit	*chuen fóon*	存款
draft	*wǒoi pīu*	匯票
exchange	*jáau wǒon*	找換
exchange rate	*wǒoi lút*	匯率
foreign currency	*ngǒi bǎi*	外幣
identification card	*sàn fán jǐng*	身份証
interest	*lēi sìk*	利息
invoice	*fāat pīu*	發票
letter of credit	*sūn yŭng jǐng*	信用証
receipt	*sàu gūi*	收據
remittance	*wǒoi fóon*	匯款
selling rate	*mǎai chùt gā*	賣出價
signature	*chìm méng*	簽名
telegraphic transfer	*dīn wǒoi*	電匯
travellers' cheque	*lǔi hang jì pīu*	旅行支票
waybill	*tai dàan*	提單
withdrawal	*tai fóon*	提款

Currency

| Australian $ | *ngō yuen* | 澳元 |
| Canadian $ | *gà na dǎai yuen* | 加拿大元 |

Deutschmarks	*mǎ hàk*	馬克
French franc	*fāat long*	法郎
HK$	*góng bāi*	港幣
Japanese yen ¥	*yāt yuen*	日元
Macau pataca M$	*po bāi*	葡幣
New Taiwan NT$	*sàn toi bāi*	新台幣
Renminbi	*yan man bāi*	人民幣
UK £	*yìng bóng*	英鎊
US$	*mēi gàm*	美金

Black Market

There is a high risk when exchanging local Renminbi on the black market. If you have exchanged money at a bank or an authorised outlet, you should always keep the official receipts for customs declaration purposes.

black market	*hàk sí*	黑市
black market rate	*hàk sí gā*	黑市價
money exchange	*wǒon chín*	換錢
official rate	*gùng gā*	公價

At the Post Office

Besides sending mail in post offices in China, you can send cables and make long-distance phone calls (although making calls from your hotel may save precious time as queues often form at the post office). Commemorative stamps and first-day covers can become good souvenirs. The main post offices in large cities are more experienced in sending international mail, especially the express and registered mails. When filling out any forms or writing addresses, write all the English words in block letters to avoid unnecessary misunderstanding.

There should be no communication problems at all in post offices in Hong Kong and Macau.

I'd like to send ... to (Australia).	ngőh séung ... hūi (ngō jàu)	我想...去(澳洲)
an aerogram	gēi gōh hong hùng yau gáan	寄個航空郵柬
a cable	dá fùng dĭn bō	打封電報
a card	gēi jèung kàat	寄張卡
a Christmas card	gēi jèung sīng dāan kàat	寄張聖誕卡
an express mail	gēi gōh fāai yau	寄個快郵
a fax	fāat yàt fān chuen jàn	發一份傳眞
a letter	gēi fùng sūn	寄封信
a parcel	gēi gōh bàau gwóh	寄個包裹
a postcard	gēi jèung ming sūn pín	寄張明信片
Are there any ... restrictions?	yắu mő ... hắan jāi ā?	有冇...限制呀?
size	dấai sāi	大細
thickness	hấu dŏ	厚度
weight	chứng lễung	重量

How much is it?
géi dòh chín ā? 幾多錢呀?

What's the weight of this?
nì gōh yắu gēi chứng ā? 呢個有幾重呀?

address	*dĕi jí*	地址
aerogram	*hong hùng yau gáan*	航空郵束
airmail	*hùng yau*	空郵
consignee	*sàu gín yan*	收件人
envelope	*sūn fùng*	信封
express mail	*fāai yau*	快郵
fax	*chuen jàn*	傳眞
general post office	*yau jīng júng gúk*	郵政總局
insurance	*bó hím*	保險
letter	*sūn*	信
letter box	*yau túng*	郵简
PO box	*yau jīng sūn sèung*	郵政信箱
parcel	*bàau gwóh*	包裹
postcard	*ming sūn pín*	明信片
postcode	*yau jīng pìn hŏ*	郵政編號
poste restante	*yau gín dŏi lĭng*	郵件待領
post office	*yau jīng gúk*	郵政局
printed matter	*yān chāat bán*	印刷品
registered mail	*gwā hŏ*	挂號
stamps	*yau pīu*	郵票
surface mail	*ping yau*	平郵
telegram	*dĭn bō*	電報
telex	*dĭn chuen*	電傳
urgent telegram	*gàp dĭn*	急電

Telephone

Using the telephone is very convenient in Hong Kong. Phone calls are reasonably priced, readily available and technologically advanced. Dialling your home country is as easy as dialling locally. Some families even set up other lines for their kids' private usage. Public phones are not as widely used as in other countries because most of the restaurants and stores allow customers to use their phones free of charge. The popularity of mobile phones is almost unequalled in the world. If you are doing business, hiring a pager or a mobile phone would be a good idea.

In China, private phones are still uncommon. Some families have to share a line and in some remote areas there may only be a few phones per village. Making a long-distance call through the operator may take you a very long time. Recently, most cities made up their own area codes, enabling people to dial directly to anywhere in the world.

I want to make a phone call
   ngőh séung dá gōh dĭn wá   我想打個電話

I want to make a phone call to
   (Canada).
   ngőh séung dá gōh dĭn wá hūi   我想打個電話去(加拿大)
   (gà na dăai)

I want to make a long-distance call to
   Beijing.
   ngőh séung dá gōh cheung to dĭn   我想打個長途電
   wá hūi (bàk gìng)   話去(北京)

I want to make an international call to
   (Canada).
   ngőh séung dá gōh gwōk jāi dĭn wá 我想打個國際電話
   hūi (gà na dăai)   去(加拿大)

What is the number?
   dĭn wá hŏ mă géi dòh hŏ ā?   電話號碼幾多號呀?

The number is ...
   dĭn wá hŏ mă hāi ...   電話號碼係...

Hello.
   wái or *wéi*   喂

Is (Mr Chan) there?
chéng màn (chan sìn sàang) hái m hái dõ ā? 請問(陳先生)喺唔喺度呀?

Can I speak to ...?
m gòi, ngõh séung wán ... tèng dĩn wá 唔該,我想搵...聽電話

area code	*dēi kùi jĩ tau*	地區字頭
beeper	*chuen fòo gèi*	傳呼機
collect call	*dūi fòng fõo fóon*	對方付款
country code	*gwõk gà pìn hõ*	國家編號
direct dial	*jĩk bõot dĩn wá*	直撥電話
directory	*dĩn wá bó*	電話部
engaged	*dĩn wá m tùng* or *jĩm sīn*	電話唔通 佔線
extension number	*nõi sín hõ mã*	內線號碼
international call	*gwõk jāi dĩn wá*	國際電話
local call	*sĩ nõi dĩn wá*	市內電話
long-distance call	*cheung to dĩn wá*	長途電話
mobile phone	*dãai gòh dãai*	大哥大
operator (in China)	*júng gèi*	總機
operator (in Hong Kong)	*jĩp sīn sàng*	接線生
pager	*chuen fòo gèi*	傳呼機
person to person	*gĩu yan dĩn wá*	叫人電話
public telephone	*gùng jūng dĩn wá*	公眾電話
return call	*fùk dĩn wá*	覆電話
station (of beeper)	*chuen fòo tòi*	傳呼台
telephone	*dĩn wá*	電話
telephone booth	*dĩn wá ting*	電話亭

telephone card	*dīn wá kàat*	電話卡
telephone charge	*dīn wá fāi*	電話費
telephone number	*dīn wá hŏ mǎ*	電話號碼
wrong number	*dá chōh dīn wá*	打錯電話

Sightseeing

Excuse me, what's this/that?
nì/góh gōh hǎi màt yé ā?   呢/嗰個係乜嘢呀?

Do you have a local map?
yǎu mŏ dòng děi děi to à?   有冇當地地圖呀?

Am I allowed to take photos here?
nì dŏ jún m jún yíng séung ā?   呢度准唔准影相呀?

What time does it (open)/(close)?
géi dím (hòi)/(sàan) moon ā?   幾點(開)/(閂)門呀?

How much is ... ?	... *géi dòh chín ā?*	...幾多錢呀?
the admission fee	*yǎp cheung fāi*	入場費
the guidebook	*sūet ming sùe*	說明書
the postcard	*ming sūn pín*	明信片
this	*nì gōh*	呢個

ancient	*góo dŏi*	古代
archaeology	*háau góo*	考古
art gallery	*měi sǔt gwóon*	美術館
building	*gīn jùk*	建築
monument	*góo jìk*	古跡
museum	*bōk màt gwóon*	博物館
old city	*gǎu sing sí*	舊城市
pagoda	*tāap*	塔
ruins	*wai jìk*	遺跡
sculpture	*sōk jěung*	塑像

sightseeing	gwòon gwòng	觀光
souvenirs	gēi nǐm bán	記念品
statues	sōk jĕung	塑像
theatre	kēk yúen	劇院

For more vocabulary of things to see, refer to Religion, page 43, the following Entertainment & Nightlife section, and the In the Country and Shopping chapters.

Entertainment & Nightlife

Most Cantonese people's philosophy of nightlife in the area is expressed in the saying 'Eating, Drinking, Playing & Enjoying', *hēk, hōt, wŏon, lŏk*, with 'eating' the most important one.

There are hundreds of discos, ballrooms, nightclubs and karaoke bars that can be quite expensive. Movies are the most popular entertainment night or day.

Sometimes traditional Peking opera, Cantonese opera, comedy, witty dialogue in different dialects are also performed. But, for locals, most exciting of all are the concerts given by popular singers, the horse races and soccer games.

Beside these, most of the local people also enjoy playing mahjong, *dá ma jĕuk*, or watching the local and international TV programs.

The well-known night views from Victoria Peak in Hong Kong, said to be worth a million dollars, are free of charge.

What's there to do in the evenings?
yĕ mǎan yáu màt yĕ jĭt mŭk ā?　今晚有乜嘢節目呀?
Is there a (karaoke) here?
nì dŏ yáu mŏ (kà làai O K) ā?　呢度有冇(卡拉ＯＫ)呀?

I'd like to see ...	ngőh séung tái ...	我想睇...
an acrobatic show	jăap gēi bíu yín	雜技表演
horse racing	páau mă	跑馬
a movie	dīn yíng	電影

I'd like to (go to) ...	ngőh séung hūi ...	我想去...
a (singing) concert	tèng yín chēung	聽演唱
join a night tour	chàam gà măan séung gwòon gwòng	參加晚上觀光

Some Useful Words

acrobat	jăap gēi	雜技
Cantonese opera	yūet kēk	粵劇
casino	dó cheung	賭場
cinema	hēi yúen	戲院
circus	mă hēi	馬戲
concert	yàm ngők wóoi	音樂會
concert hall	yàm ngők tèng	音樂廳
dance	tīu mő	跳舞
disco	dìk sī gò	的士高
dog racing	páau gáu	跑狗
floor show	fòh sò	科騷
folk dance	tó fùng mő	土風舞
karaoke	kà làai O K	卡拉 O K
local opera	dēi fòng hēi	地方戲
magic show	mòh sūt bíu yín	魔術表演
movie	dīn yíng	電影
nightclub	yé júng wóoi	夜總會
nightlife	yé sàn wőot	夜生活
night tour	măan séung gwòon gwòng	晚上觀光

Peking opera	*gìng kēk*	京劇
song & dance troupe	*gòh mő tuen*	歌舞團
theatre	*kēk yúen*	劇院
witty dialogue	*sēung sìng*	相聲

Musical Instruments

China has developed many musical instruments over thousands of years, many of which have been adopted by the Cantonese people. Traditionally, bronze bells (similar to chimes) were the most popular instruments used in the Emperor's palace. Others include woodwind instruments called *sìu* and *dēk*, which are very similar to flutes, and the *sàng*, which is a gourd-shaped hand-held musical instrument with a row of reed pipes.

Common stringed instruments include the butterfly harp, *yeung kám*, the Er-hu, *yĭ wóo*, and Pi-pa, *pei pá*. The *jàng* is a flat stringed zither with thirteen strings, similar to the Japanese *koto*. Woodwinds and strings form the main portion of traditional Cantonese music. Played together with violins and other Western musical instruments, modern Cantonese music is further enriched.

Drums, *góo*, gongs, *loh,* and cymbals, *bāt,* are played during the New Year celebrations and for other festive events. One characteristic of traditional Chinese music is its omission of the fourth note of the scale, fa, and the seventh note, ti, leaving only do, re, mi, so and la – the pentatonic scale.

I like Chinese music.
   ngőh jùng yī jùng gwōk yàm ngōk   我中意中國音樂
Which musical instrument do you play?
   néi wáan màt yĕ ngōk hēi ā?   你玩乜嘢樂器呀?

Signs

提防惡犬	BEWARE OF DOGS
提防小手	BEWARE OF PICKPOCKETS
危險	DANGER
緊急	EMERGENCY
出口	EXIT
靜	KEEP QUIET
不准進入	NO ADMITTANCE
不准駛入	NO ENTRY
不准用閃光燈	NO FLASHLIGHTS
不准停車	NO PARKING
禁止攝影	NO PHOTOGRAPHY
禁止吸煙	NO SMOKING
禁區	RESTRICTED AREA

看

To look

In the Country

Weather

It's important to know the weather forecast before you travel into the country as the weather may change dramatically from one moment to another. Make sure you are fully equipped and have enough clothes and rain gear. Sunglasses and sunscreen are a necessity when travelling in the tropical areas.

What's the weather like today/
   tomorrow?
   gàm/tìng yăt tìn hēi dím ā?   今/聽日天氣點呀?
The weather is nice today.
   gàm yăt tìn hēi hó hó   今日天氣好好
Will it rain tomorrow?
   tìng yăt wōoi m wōoi lŏk yŭe ā?   聽日會唔會落雨呀?

It's hot.	*hó yĭt*	好熱
It's raining	*lŏk gán yŭe*	落緊雨
It's fine.	*hó hó tìn*	好好天

bright	*gwòng măang*	光猛
clear	*ching lŏng*	晴朗
cloud	*wan*	雲
cloudy	*yàm tìn*	陰天
cyclone	*suen fùng*	旋風
dark	*ngām*	暗
dew	*lŏ súi*	露水
evening glow	*măan ha*	晚霞

fine weather	*hó tìn*	好天
flood	*hung súi*	洪水
fog	*mõ*	霧
frost	*sèung*	霜
hail	*bõk*	雹
heavy rain	*dãai yűe*	大雨
humid	*ngāi gũk*	翳侷
lightning	*sím dĩn*	閃電
mist	*ha*	霞
mud	*nai*	泥
rain	*yűe*	雨
raining	*lõk yűe*	落雨
rainbow	*chói hung*	彩虹
rainy season	*yűe gwāi*	雨季
shower	*jãau yűe*	驟雨
sky	*tìn*	天
snow	*sūet*	雪
snowing	*lõk sūet*	落雪
storm	*bõ fùng yűe*	暴風雨
sunny	*hó yeung gwòng*	好陽光
sunrise	*yãt chùt*	日出
sunset	*yãt lõk*	日落
thunder	*lui*	雷
tornado	*lung gúen fùng*	龍卷風
tropics	*yĩt dãai*	熱帶
typhoon	*toi fùng*	颱風
very cold	*hó dũng*	好凍
very cool	*hó leung*	好涼
very hot	*hó yĩt*	好熱
very warm	*hó nuẽn*	好暖
very windy	*hó dãai fùng*	好大風

weather	*tìn hēi*	天氣
weather forecast	*tìn hēi yūe bō*	天氣預報
wet	*chiu sàp*	潮濕
wind	*fùng*	風

Camping & Day Trips

Have you brought the ...?
dāi jóh ... mēi ā? 帶咗...未呀?

Do you need to bring the ...?
yīu m yīu dāi ... ā? 要唔要帶...呀?

When do we go?
géi si chùt fāat ā? 幾時出發呀?

Where do we meet?
ngóh dēi hái bìn dō jǎap hǎp ā? 我哋喺邊度集合呀?

We will come back ...	*ngóh dēi ... fàan lai*	我哋...番嚟
at (9) o'clock tonight	*gàm mǎan (gáu) dím jùng*	今晚(九)點鐘
tomorrow	*tìng yāt*	聽日
tomorrow evening	*tìng mǎan*	聽晚
the day after tomorrow	*hǎu yāt*	後日

backpack	*bōoi nong*	背囊
boots	*cheung hèuh*	長靴
camping	*lōe ying*	露營
campsite	*ying dēi*	營地
compass	*jí naam jàm*	指南針
departure time	*chùt fāat si gāan*	出發時間
insect repellent	*màn pā súi*	蚊怕水

kettle	*súi wóo*	水壺
knife	*dò*	刀
rope	*sing sōk*	繩索
shelter	*bĕi yŭe tìng*	避雨亭
sleeping bag	*sŭi dói*	睡袋
sunscreen	*tāai yeung yau*	太陽油
telescope	*mŏng yŭen gēng*	望遠鏡
tent	*jĕung mōk*	帳幕
torch (flashlight)	*sáu dĭn túng*	手電筒
walkie talkie	*dūi góng gèi*	對講機

Along the Way

The highlights of Guangdong province and Canton (Guangzhou) don't include any spectacular scenery. The main attractions are the many historical monuments, temples of different religions, street markets and, of course, the food. However there are opportunities to relax on beaches, cruise on the Pearl River and go walking in the White Cloud Hills, Lotus Mountain and Yuexiu Park.

The magnificent scenery in Guangxi has long been a source of traditional ink paintings, particularly around Guilin and Yangshuo, and this is where you'll get the most out of trekking and river excursions.

In Hong Kong, there still remain a few traditional walled villages called *wai*. They are completely surrounded by high, strong brick walls, with narrow entrances, originally built for protection against invaders. Away from the city you can visit a fishing village, go hiking in the parks or visit the islands.

Macau is like a model of what happens when a European city is combined with the Chinese culture.

Where are we?
nì dõ hái bìn dõ ā?

呢度喺邊度呀?

Are there any famous monuments here?
nì dõ yǎu màt yẽ ming sīng góo jìk ā?

呢度有乜名勝古跡呀?

Can you please tell me how to get to ... ?
chéng mǎn ... dím hūi ā?

請問...點去呀?

What will we past on the way?
wōoi gìng gwōh màt yẽ dẽi fòng ā?

會經過乜嘢地方呀?

How far is it from here to ...?
chéng mǎn ... jūng yǎu géi yúen ā?

請問...重有幾遠呀?

Are there any things to see here/there?
nì/góh dõ yǎu màt yẽ tái ā?

呢/嗰度有乜嘢睇呀?

Let's take a rest here.
ngõh dẽi hái nì dõ yàu sìk yàt jãn

我哋喺呢度休息一陣

Can I have a cup of (water)/(tea)?
chéng mǎn hóh m̀ hóh yẽ béi bòoi (súi)/(cha) ngõh ā?

請問可唔可以俾杯 (水)/(茶)我呀?

What's (this)/(that)?
(nì)/(góh) dì hãi màt yẽ lai gā?

呢/嗰啲係乜嘢嚟㗎?

Directions

direction	*fòng hēung*	方向
east	*dùng*	東
south	*naam*	南
west	*sài*	西
north	*bàk*	北
southeast	*dùng naam*	東南
northwest	*sài bàk*	西北
uphill	*séung sàan*	上山

downhill	*lŏk sàan*	落山
left	*jóh bìn*	左便
right	*yău bìn*	右便

Which direction is the ...?
   ... hái bìn yàt gōh fòng hēung ā?   ... 喺邊一個方向呀?

Useful Words

agriculture	*nung yĭp*	農業
bay	*wàan*	灣
beach	*sà tàan*	沙灘
cave	*sàan lùng*	山窿
cliff	*yuen ngaai*	懸崖
country	*gàau ngōi*	郊外
country park	*gàau yĕ gùng yúen*	郊野公園
creek	*kài gāan*	溪澗
desert	*sà mŏk*	沙漠
earth	*dĕi*	地
earthquake	*dĕi jān*	地震
farm	*nung cheung*	農場
farmer	*nung man*	農民
fishery	*yue yĭp*	漁業
forest	*sàm lam*	森林
forestry	*lam yĭp*	林業
gap	*sàan hăap*	山峽
grassy plains	*chó yuen*	草原
harbour	*góng háu*	港口
high plateau	*gò yuen*	高原
hill	*sàan gòng*	山崗
hot spring	*wàn chuen*	溫泉

island	*dó*	島
jungle	*chung lam*	叢林
lake	*woo*	湖
landslide	*sàan bàng*	山崩
lookout	*liu mŏng toi*	瞭望台
map	*dēi to*	地圖
mountain	*sàan*	山
mountain range	*sàan māk*	山脈
mountain trail	*sàan lŏ*	山路
mudslide	*sàan nai kìng sē*	山泥傾瀉
ocean	*hói yeung*	海洋
park	*gùng yúen*	公園
pavilion	*leung tíng*	涼亭
peak	*sàan déng*	山頂
peninsula	*bōon dó*	半島
pond	*chi tong*	池塘
public toilet	*gùng chī*	公廁
ricefield	*dŏ tin*	稻田
river	*hoh*	河
road	*dŏ lŏ*	道路
rock	*ngaam sēk*	岩石
sea	*hói*	海
soil	*nai tó*	泥土
stone	*sēk*	石
swamp	*júu jăak*	沼澤
tide	*chiu jīk*	潮汐
valley	*sàan gùk*	山谷
village	*hèung chùen*	鄉村
waterfall	*bŭk bō*	瀑布
wave (at beach)	*lŏng*	浪
well	*jéng*	井

Animals

bat	*pìn fùk*	蝙蝠
camel	*lōk toh*	駱駝
cat	*màau*	貓
cow	*ngau*	牛
deer	*lúk*	鹿
dog	*gáu*	狗
domestic animals	*gà chùk*	家畜
elephant	*jēung*	象
fox	*woo léi*	狐狸
goat	*sàan yeung*	山羊
hare	*yé tō*	野兔
horse	*mǎ*	馬
leopard	*pāau*	豹
lion	*sì jí*	獅子
monkey	*mǎ làu*	馬騮
mouse	*lő súe*	老鼠
ox	*gùng ngau*	公牛
panda	*hung màau*	熊貓
pig	*jùe*	豬
rabbit	*tō*	兔
sheep	*yeung*	羊
squirrel	*chung súe*	松鼠
tiger	*lő fóo*	老虎
wild animal	*yé sàng dǔng māt*	野生動物
wolf	*long*	狼

Birds

birds (long tail)	*nǐu*	鳥
birds (short tail)	*jēuk*	雀
chicken	*gài*	雞

crane	hŏk	鶴
crow	wòo ngà	烏鴉
duck	ngāap	鴨
eagle	yìng	鷹
goose	ngóh	鵝
lark	wan jéuk	雲雀
parrot	yìng mŏ	鸚鵡
peacock	húng jēuk	孔雀
penguin	kĕi ngŏh	企鵝
pigeon	bāak gāp	白鴿
rooster	gài gùng	雞公
seagull	hói ngàu	海鷗
sparrow	ma jēuk	麻雀
swallow	yīn jí	燕子

Marine Creatures

abalone	bàau yue	鮑魚
carp	léi yúe	鯉魚
crab	hăai	蟹
dace	leng yúe	鯪魚
dolphin	hói tuen	海豚
eel	maan	鰻魚
fish	yúe	魚
freshwater fish	tăam súi yúe	淡水魚
globe fish	gài pŏ yúe	雞泡魚
jellyfish	bāak jā	白鮓
prawn	dāai hà	大蝦
saltwater fish	hăam súi yúe	鹹水魚
sea cucumber	hói sàm	海參
sea horse	hói mă	海馬

sea urchin	*hói dáam*	海膽
seal	*hói pāau*	海豹
shark	*sà yúe*	鯊魚
shrimp	*hà*	蝦
skate fish	*mòh gwái yúe*	魔鬼魚
tropical fish	*yĭt dāai yúe*	熱帶魚
whale	*king yue*	鯨魚

Insects & Reptiles

ant	*mǎ ngǎi*	螞蟻
bee	*māt fùng*	蜜蜂
beetle	*gāap chung*	甲蟲
butterfly	*woo dĭp*	蝴蝶
centipede	*ng gùng*	蜈蚣
cobra	*ngǎan gēng se*	眼鏡蛇
cockroach	*gǎat jǎat*	甲由
crocodile	*ngŏk yue*	鱷魚
earthworm	*yàu yǎn*	蚯蚓
fly	*wòo yìng*	烏蠅
frog	*tin gài*	田雞
lice	*sàt*	虱
lizard	*sìk yĭk*	蜥蜴
mosquito	*màn*	蚊
moth	*ngoh*	蛾
poisonous snake	*dŭk se*	毒蛇
rattlesnake	*héung měi se*	響尾蛇
scorpion	*dŭk kīt*	毒蝎
silkworm	*chaam chúng*	蠶蟲
snake	*se*	蛇
spider	*jì jùe*	蜘蛛
termite	*bǎak ngǎi*	白蟻

| turtle | *gwài* | 龜 |
| wasp | *yế fùng* | 野蜂 |

Plants & Flowers

In rural China, you will often see village people gathering and socialising under the huge banyan trees after dinner. These gatherings are so common and popular that the banyan tree, *yung sũe tau*, has become a symbol for social gatherings.

The beautiful purple flower, *Bauhinia blakeana*, from the Hong Kong orchid tree, is Hong Kong's floral emblem.

bamboo	*jùk*	竹
banyan tree	*yung sũe*	榕樹
Bauhinia	*yeung jí gìng*	洋紫荊
bonsai	*poon jòi*	盆栽
cactus	*sìn yan jéung*	仙人掌
camellia	*cha fà*	茶花
camphor tree	*jèung tree*	樟樹
carnation	*hòng nǎi hìng* or *dìng hèung*	康乃馨 丁香
cherry blossom	*yìng fà*	櫻花
chrysanthemum	*gùk fà*	菊花
cotton tree	*mǔk min sũe*	木棉樹
cypress	*pāak sũe*	柏樹
elm	*yue sũe*	榆樹
flower	*fà*	花
forest	*sàm lam*	森林
forget-me-not	*mo mong ngốh*	毋忘我
gladiolus	*gĩm laan*	劍蘭
grass	*chó*	草

Hong Kong orchid tree	*yeung jí gìng sūe*	洋紫荊樹
jasmine	*mõot léi fà*	茉莉花
jonquil	*súi sìn fà*	水仙花
judas tree	*jí gìng*	紫荊
leaf	*yīp*	葉
lily	*bāak hãp*	百合
locust tree	*waai sūe*	槐樹
lotus	*lin fà* or *hoh fà*	蓮花/荷花
maple	*fùng sūe*	楓樹
oleander	*gāap jùk to*	夾竹桃
orchid	*laan fà*	蘭花
palm	*jùng lui*	棕櫚
peach flower	*to fà*	桃花
peony	*mãau dàan*	牡丹
petal	*fà fáan*	花瓣
petunia	*hìn ngau fà*	牽牛花
pine	*chung sūe*	松樹
plum flower	*mooi fà*	梅花
root	*gàn*	根
rose	*mooi gwāi*	玫瑰
shrub	*gwōon mūk*	灌木
stem	*gīng*	莖
sugar cane	*gàm jē*	甘蔗
tree	*sūe*	樹
white champak	*bãak laan*	白蘭
willow	*yeung lãu*	楊柳

Astronomical & Related Terms

| Altair | *ngau long* | 牛郎 |
| Big Dipper | *bàk dáu chàt sìng* | 北斗七星 |

comet	*sō bá sìng*	掃把星
constellation	*sìng jŏh*	星座
Earth	*dēi kau*	地球
full moon	*mŏon yūet*	滿月
Jupiter	*mŭk sìng*	木星
lunar eclipse	*yūet sĩk*	月蝕
Mars	*fóh sìng*	火星
Mercury	*súi sìng*	水星
meteor	*lau sìng*	流星
Milky Way	*ngan hoh*	銀河
Moon	*yūet*	月
nebula	*sìng wan*	星雲
new moon	*sàn yūet*	新月
Orion	*lĩp wŏo sìng jŏh*	獵戶星座
planet	*hang sìng*	行星
Polaris	*bàk gĩk sìng*	北極星
Saturn	*tó sìng*	土星
solar eclipse	*yăt sĩk*	日蝕
Southern Cross	*naam săp jĩ sìng*	南十字星
star	*sìng*	星
Sun	*tāai yeung*	太陽
universe	*yūe jău*	宇宙
Venus	*gàm sìng*	金星
Vega	*jìk nũi*	織女

Country Parks in Hong Kong

There are four main types of country parks in Hong Kong. Some are specifically for recreational purposes, with playgrounds, lookouts, pavilions, trails for bush-walking, barbecue facilities, picnic areas and even campsites. Rangers patrol the areas and are there to assist you if any problems may occur.

There are other parks which accommodate more serious walkers, rock climbers and hikers. The popular cliff of the Lion Rock is one of the steepest cliffs in South-East Asia.

The third type is the wildlife observations. Mai Po Nature Reserve is a world-famous bird sanctuary, and permission is needed before you are allowed entry to it.

The last type is the reserves that are used mainly for scientific research, where plants and animals are kept in their natural environments and access is restricted.

Generally, the facilities in Hong Kong's parks are outstanding. They provide visitors with detailed maps and are well signposted.

There are also several trails in the country parks which you may like to try. The MacLehose Trail, which is 100 km long, the Lantau Trail, stretching 70 km and Hong Kong Trail, a modest 50 km. All the trails are separated into sections, depending on how far you wish to walk. The views are magnificent – in places you are likely to enjoy the oceanic scenes on one side of the trail while overlooking the modern city on the other.

country park	gàau yéˊ gùng yúen	郊野公園
Ocean Park	hói yeung gùng yúen	海洋公園
sanctuary	bó wǒo kùi	保護區
Mai Po Nature Reserve	mǎi bō jî yin wǒo leî kùi	米埔自然護理區
MacLehose Trail	mǎk leî hǒ gīng	麥理浩徑
Lantau Trail	fûng wong gīng	鳳凰徑
Hong Kong Trail	góng dó gīng	港島徑
section	dũen	段

Food

There is an old saying in Chinese, *man yǐ sīk wai sìn*, literally meaning 'eating is the people's first priority'. To Cantonese people, eating is not only a need, it is an art. On special occasions, they may spend hours, days or even weeks preparing extravagant dishes. Over many centuries the Chinese have perfected their own unique style of cooking which they regard as a fine art. Cantonese cuisine has largely inherited the Chinese cuisine's extensive range of cooking styles and methods, and the Cantonese are known for their ability to cook virtually anything. The dishes are many and varied. Unlike many other national cuisines, there isn't one dish that has captured the essence of the cuisine. However, there is one distinctive characteristic of the Cantonese style: all the ingredients in the dishes keep their original flavours.

Hong Kong's convenient location, being the centre point of east and west, north and south in Asia, is a significant reason for its inhabitants' multicultural eating habits. Transporting of ingredients is convenient and this, in turn, attracts chefs from China and all over the world. Many visitors consider Hong Kong to be a food paradise, and Cantonese people agree. Eating is a very significant part of their lives. For many of the island's inhabitants, Cantonese meals are social events. You wouldn't, therefore, expect to experience the tranquillity of a Western restaurant in a Cantonese eatery.

breakfast	*jó chàan*	早餐
lunch	*ng̃ chàan*	午餐
dinner	*mãan chàan*	晚餐

afternoon tea	*hā nḡ cha*	下午茶
midnight snack	*sìu yé*	宵夜
snack	*síu sĩk*	小食
tea	*cha dím*	茶點

Restaurants

It's said that 'wherever there are people, there is going to be a Chinese person, wherever there is a Chinese person, there is going to be a Chinese restaurant'. Hong Kong not only has many restaurants that specialise in the cuisines of the regions of China, it also has restaurants that specialise in other nations' cuisines, from Mediterranean to Japanese dishes.

The Cantonese people go to restaurants on all occasions, from weddings to funerals, birthday parties to farewell parties.

Eateries

bar	*jáu bà*	酒吧
canteen	*fāan tong*	飯堂
Chinese restaurant	*jáu lau* or	酒樓
	jáu gà	酒家
Chinese tea house	*cha lau*	茶樓
coffee house	*gā fè tèng*	咖啡廳
floating restaurant	*hói sìn fóng*	海鮮舫
food centre	*yám sĩk jùng sàm*	飲食中心
food court/street	*sĩk gàai*	食街

herb teahouse	*leung cha pó*	涼茶舖
kiosk	*síu sĭk dīm*	小食店
lounge	*jáu long*	酒廊
nightclub	*yĕ júng wóoi*	夜總會
pub	*jàu bà*	酒吧
restaurant	*chàan tèng*	餐廳
seafood restaurant	*hói sìn jáu gà*	海鮮酒家
stall	*dāai paai dōng*	大牌檔
vegetarian restaurant	*jàai chōi gwóon* or *sō chōi gwóon*	齋菜館 素菜館
VIP room	*gwāi bàn tèng*	貴賓廳
Western-style restaurant	*sài chàan tèng*	西餐廳

Chinese Regional Cuisines

| I want to go to a restaurant with ... | *ngŏh séung hūi sĭk ...* | 我想去食... |

Beijing food	*gìng chōi*	京菜
Cantonese food	*gwóng dùng chōi* or *yŭet chōi*	廣東菜 粵菜
Chaozhou food	*chiu jàu chōi*	潮州菜
Chinese food	*jùng gwōk chōi*	中國菜
eastern Chinese food	*waai yeung chōi*	淮揚菜
Hunan food	*sèung chōi*	湘菜
Kejia food	*dùng gòng chōi* or *hāak gà chōi*	東江菜 客家菜
northern Chinese food	*bàk fòng chōi*	北方菜

Shandong food	*sàan dùng chōi*	山東菜
Shanghai food	*sĕung hói chōi*	上海菜
Sichuan food	*chùen chōi*	川菜
Taiwanese food	*toi wàan chōi*	台灣菜

Other National Cuisines

fast food	*fāai chàan*	快餐
French food	*fāat gwōk chōi*	法國菜
Indian food	*yān dŏ chōi*	印度菜
Japanese food	*yāt bóon lĭu lĕī*	日本料理
Japanese teppanyaki	*yāt bóon tīt báan sìu*	日本鐵板燒
Korean food	*hon gwōk chōi*	韓國菜
South-East Asian food	*naam yéung chōi*	南洋菜
Thai food	*tāai gwōk chōi*	泰國菜
Vietnamese food	*yŭet naam chōi*	越南菜
Western food	*sài chàan*	西餐

At the Restaurant

A table for ... please
   m gòi ... wái   唔該∶..位

Can I see the menu please?
   m gói béi gōh chàan páai tái há   唔該俾個餐牌睇吓

Do you have an English menu?
   yáu mŏ yìng mán chàan páai ā?   有冇英文餐牌呀?

I would like the set menu please.
   ngŏh yīu gōh tō chàan   我要個套餐

Can you recommend any dishes?
   yáu màt yĕ hó gāai sĭu ā?   有乜嘢好介紹呀?

Are the (fish/prawns/crabs) fresh
   today?
   *gàm yāt dì (yúe/hà/hāai) lēng m
   lēng ā?*

今日啲（魚/蝦/蟹）
靚唔靚呀？

Please give me a knife and a fork.
   m gòi béi ngő yàt fōo dò chà

唔該俾我一副刀叉

The bill please.
   m gòi maai dàan

唔該埋單

captain (head waiter)	*bő jéung*	部長
chef	*dăai chúe*	大廚
waiter	*fóh gēi*	伙記
waitress	*síu jé*	小姐

Staples

noodles	*mīn*	麵
rice	*fāan*	飯
rice noodle rolls	*chéung fán*	腸粉
rice noodles	*làai fán*	瀨粉
rice noodles (shredded)	*hóh fán*	河粉
rice vermicelli	*măi fán*	米粉

Vegetarian Meals

Traditionally, the only reason for vegetarian habits was for religious purposes, not because the Chinese wanted to eat healthy
food. The monasteries are the first true vegetarian restaurants,
providing visitors with vegetarian dishes most of which resemble

meat in color, shape and even taste, although they are still strictly vegetarian. This tradition goes back more than a thousand years!

Nowadays, as more and more people become vegetarian, more and more vegetarian restaurants are being established. Due to the influence of Western culture, you can now find health food shops scattered all around Hong Kong.

I am a vegetarian.
   ngőh sīk jàai   我食齋
I don't eat meat.
   ngőh m sīk yūk lūi   我唔食肉類
I like vegetarian food.
   ngőh jùng yī sīk jàai chōi   我中意食齋菜

health food	*gīn hòng sīk bán*	健康食品
vegetarian food	*jàai* or	齋
	jàai chōi	齋菜
vegetarian restaurant	*sō chōi gwóon*	素菜館

Breakfast

A huge variety of breakfasts exist. You can have the convenient takeaway at McDonald's, buy traditional rice porridge from the stalls, *dăai paai dōng*, try a morning yum cha or enjoy a continental breakfast at any hotel restaurant.

Cantonese people don't normally eat rice for breakfast, unless it's in the form of congee (rice porridge).

Chinese Breakfast

dim sim	*dím sàm*	點心
fried bread stick	*yau jā gwái* or	油炸鬼
	yau tíu	油條

rice noodles with shrimp	*hà chéung*	蝦腸
rice noodles with beef	*ngau chéung*	牛腸
rice porridge	*jùk*	粥
rice porridge with beef	*ngau yūk jùk*	牛肉粥
sesame seed pancake	*sìu béng*	燒餅
steamed bun	*bàau*	飽
soya bean milk	*dāu jèung*	豆漿

Western Breakfast

bacon	*yìn yūk*	煙肉
bread	*mìn bàau*	麵飽
coffee	*gā fè*	咖啡
fried egg	*jìn dáan*	煎蛋
ham	*fóh túi*	火腿
juice	*gwóh jàp*	果汁
milk	*ngau nǎai*	牛奶
tea	*hung cha*	紅茶
toast	*dòh sí*	多士

Lunch

Cantonese people's favourite lunch is, you guessed it, yum cha! Another section of this chapter has been devoted to this important aspect of the art of eating.

Other people may opt for a simple, hot lunch, a plate of rice with something on the top or maybe fried noodles, available from fast food shops. The lunches are relatively light and quick.

noodles in soup	*tòng mīn*	湯麵
set menu	*tō chàan*	套餐
set menu (full course)	*chuen chàan*	全餐
set menu (ordinary)	*seung chàan*	常餐

Yum Cha

I want to (go to/for) yum cha.

ngőh séung hūi yám cha   我想去飲茶

The above is the favourite saying of the ever-hungry Cantonese people. *Yám cha* literally means 'drink tea', but it implies eating dim sims and other food while the tea is served. It's an earlier form of yum cha to what is now a feast on dim sims. Yum cha is a hot meal (breakfast, brunch or lunch, but not dinner) that is comprised mostly of dim sims and not much rice. It is so popular among Cantonese people it has become the symbol of socialising. People go to yum cha for breakfast, lunch, business deals and whatever reasons they can think of, not just for the meal.

Unlike Western restaurants, Cantonese eateries are usually crowded and extremely noisy. Expect to wait for a table on arrival, even if you have booked one. Sometimes you may even be asked to share a table, but this is an exception rather than the rule. One Cantonese custom that you will easily get used to; they fight to pay for the meal! It's an amusing scene. The Cantonese will go to almost any lengths to be the host. Sometimes they even sneak to the reception to pay the bill!

savoury	*haam dím sàm*	鹹點心
sweet	*tim dím sàm*	甜點心

Tea

Ordering tea at yum cha is a must. There are many types of teas that exist, all tasting distinctly different. Don't be afraid to try new flavours. Refer to the Hot Drinks section in this chapter.

I would like a pot of (Jasmine) tea please.
m gói, ngőh yīu yàt woo   唔該, 我要一壺
(hèung pín) cha   (香片)茶

Savoury – Steamed

[Steamed buns filled with ...]

assorted meat	*dãai bàau*	大飽
barbecue pork	*chà sìu bàau*	叉燒飽
chicken	*gài bàau*	雞飽
Chinese sausage	*lãap cheung gúen*	臘腸卷

[Dumplings filled with ...]

bamboo shoots, pork and prawn	*sìn hà fán gwóh*	鮮蝦粉果
coriander and pork	*hèung sài gáau*	香茜餃
crab, pork and prawn	*hãai wong sìu máai*	蟹黃燒賣
seafood	*hói sìn gáau*	海鮮餃
shark fin	*yue chī gáau*	魚翅餃
shrimp	*hà gáau*	蝦餃
soup	*gwōon tòng gáau*	灌湯餃

[Rice-noodle rolls filled with ...]

barbecue pork	*chà sìu cheung fán*	叉燒腸粉
beef	*ngau yũk cheung fán*	牛肉腸粉
fried bread stick	*jā lếung*	炸兩
prawns	*hà cheung fán*	蝦腸粉

Here are some more savoury steamed dishes:

beef balls	*gòn jìng ngau yŭk*	干蒸牛肉
chicken claws with black bean sauce	*sī jàp fūng jáau*	豉汁鳳爪
chicken wrap	*gài jāat*	雞紮
pork chop with black bean sauce	*sī jàp paai gwàt*	豉汁排骨
rice porridge	*jùk*	粥
shark's fin soup	*wóon jái chī*	碗仔翅
squid with black bean sauce	*sī jàp sìn yáu*	豉汁鮮魷
sticky rice dumplings	*nŏh măi gài*	糯米雞
webbed feet wrap	*ngāap gēuk jāat*	鴨腳紮

Savoury – Fried & Deep-Fried

dumpling with taro fillings	*wŏo gōk*	芋角
egg-shaped dumpling with fillings	*haam súi gōk*	鹹水角
pan stick fried dumpling	*wòh tīp*	鍋貼
rice noodle roll	*gìn cheung fán*	煎腸粉
sesame prawn on toast	*jì ma hà*	芝麻蝦
spring roll	*jā chùn gúen*	炸春卷
taro cake	*wŏo táu gò*	芋頭糕
turnip cake	*loh bāak gò*	蘿蔔糕

Sweets – Steamed

buns with egg yolk and cream	*năai wong bàau*	奶黃飽
buns with lotus seed filling	*lin yung bàau*	蓮蓉飽
buns with sesame seed filling	*ma yung bàau*	麻蓉飽
Malaysian-style sponge cake	*mă làai gò*	馬拉糕
sponge cake	*sùng gò*	鬆糕

Sweets – Fried & Deep-Fried

cakes with water chestnut	*mă tái gò*	馬蹄糕
sesame ball	*jìn dùi*	煎堆
toffee apple	*băt sì ping gwóh*	拔絲萍果

Sweets – Soup

almond fruit jelly	*hăng yan dău fŏo*	杏仁豆腐
almond milk	*hăng yan cha*	杏仁茶
beancurd jelly	*dău fŏo fà*	豆腐花
Chinese jelly (agar-agar)	*leung fán*	涼粉
red bean soup	*hung dáu sà*	紅豆沙
sago milk with coconut	*ye jàp sài măi lŏ*	椰汁西米露
sago milk with honeydew melon	*măt gwà sài măi lŏ*	蜜瓜西米露
sesame seed dumpling	*jì ma tòng yúen*	芝麻湯丸

Sweets – Others

coconut custard jelly	*ye jàp gò*	椰汁糕
coconut tart	*ye tàat*	椰撻
custard tart	*dàan tàat*	蛋撻
fruit jelly	*jàap gwóh jè léi*	雜果這喱
fruit pudding	*jàap gwóh bō dìn*	雜果布甸
mango pudding	*mòng gwóh bō dìn*	芒果布甸
sago pudding	*sài mái bō dìn*	西米布甸
sesame roll	*jì ma gúen*	芝麻卷

Afternoon Tea

The British tradition of an afternoon tea at about 3.15pm is a must for most people in Hong Kong. It could range from a cup of tea and some biscuits, to a bowl of noodles at the restaurant or a mini-lunch.

I would like a ...	*ngőh yīu ...*	我要...
barbecue pork bun	*chà sìu bàau*	叉燒飽
biscuit	*béng gòn*	餅干
bread	*mǐn bàau*	麵飽
cake	*sài béng*	西餅
club sandwich	*gùng sì sàam man jī*	公司三文治
coconut tart	*ye tàat*	椰撻
cream cake	*gēi lím dàan gò*	忌廉蛋糕
croissant	*ngau gók bàau*	牛角飽
dessert	*tim bán*	甜品
dim sim	*dím sàm*	點心
dinner roll	*chàan bàau*	餐飽
dumpling	*gáau jí*	餃子

egg cake	*dāan gò*	蛋糕
egg tart	*dāan tàat*	蛋撻
French toast	*sài dòh sí*	西多士
garlic bread	*sūen yung bàau*	蒜茸飽
hamburger	*hōn bó bàau*	漢堡飽
hot cake	*hàk gìk*	克戟
ice cream	*sūet gò*	雪糕
noodles with shrimp dumplings	*wan tàn mīn*	雲吞麵
noodles with dumplngs	*súi gáau mīn*	水餃麵
omelette	*ngàm līt*	奄列
pancake	*bŏk béng*	薄餅
pizza	*yī dāai lĕi sìu béng*	意大利燒餅
rice porridge	*jùk*	粥
sandwich	*sàam man jī*	三文治
sweet bread	*tim mīn bàau*	甜麵飽
toast	*dòh sí*	多士

Dinner

Dinner is considered to be the most important meal of the day. Many Cantonese people believe that you should always go to bed on a full stomach. Here are some common dishes:

bāak fà yeung dāai jí　百花釀帶子
  Grilled, stuffed scallops in white sauce.

bàk gìng tin ngāap　北京塡鴨
  Also known as Peking Duck. The crispy skin of the fresh roasted duck is sliced and served in pancakes with leek or cucumber and sauce.

chèng jìu ngau yūk 青椒牛肉
Shredded beef stir-fried with capsicum.

chìng jìng yúe 清蒸魚
Steamed whole fish.

chōi yűen pa ngāap 菜遠扒鴨
Braised duck and green vegetables.

chōi yűen sĕk bàan kau 菜遠石斑球
Garoupa (fish) balls and green vegetables.

dăai leung wòh sìu ngāap 大良窩燒鴨
Deep-fried, stuffed duck in crabmeat sauce.

gèung chùng hăai 薑蔥蟹
Baked crab in ginger and spring onion sauce.

gèung chùng ngau yūk 薑蔥牛肉
Beef stir-fried with ginger and spring onion.

gìng dò gwàt 京都骨
Spare rib, Beijing-style.

gòn sìu ming hà 干燒明蝦
Dried-fried spicy king prawns.

gòo lò yūk 咕老肉
Sweet and sour pork.

gūk hăai gōi 焗蟹蓋
Crabmeat crumbs, deep-fried in the shell.

gùng bó gài dìng 宮保雞丁
Diced chicken stir-fried with peanuts, pepper and chilli flakes.

hàt yì gài 乞兒雞
Also known as 'beggar's chicken'. The whole chicken is rubbed with spices and stuffed. It is wrapped in lotus leaves and clay-dough, then baked.

ho yau bàau pó 蠔油鮑脯
Abalone in oyster sauce.

ho yau ngau yŭk　蠔油牛肉
　　Sliced beef in oyster sauce.

hói sìn jĕuk chaau　海鮮雀巢
　　A combination of prawns, scallops and fish in a fried potato
　　or taro tray that resembles a bird's nest.

jā jí gài　炸子雞
　　Deep-fried chicken.

jā sàang ho　炸生蠔
　　Deep-fried oysters.

jā sín năai　炸鮮奶
　　Deep-fried milk mixture with egg white.

jí bàau gwàt/gài　紙包骨/雞
　　Spare rib/chicken wrapped with rice paper.

jìn yĕung dāu fŏo　煎釀豆腐
　　Grilled fish, prawns or meat stuffed in beancurd.

jìu yim sìn yáu　椒鹽鮮魷
　　Fried calamari in spicy peppery salt.

ké jàp hà lùk　茄汁蝦碌
　　Broiled king prawn in tomato sauce.

ma poh dāu fŏo　麻婆豆腐
　　Braised beancurd with minced beef and chillies.

ngan woo bāak fà pó　銀湖百花脯
　　Prawn patties in crabmeat sauce.

sàang chōi bàau　生菜包
　　Lettuce roll with minced pork or seafood.

sĕung tòng gài　上湯雞
　　Chicken boiled in stock soup.

sĭ jăp gŭk hăai　豉汁焗蟹
　　Baked crab in black bean sauce.

wooi wòh yŭk　回鍋肉
　　Broiled pork slice cooked with garlic, peppers and soya bean sauce.

yue hèung ké jí　魚香茄子
　　Chunks of eggplant and pork batons sautéed in a spicy vinegar sauce.

Banquet

The following is a list of the more common entrées or appetisers used at Chinese and Western banquets. For main dishes, refer to both the Dinner and Main Dishes sections in this chapter.

appetiser	*chàan chin síu sĭk*	餐前小食
Chinese combination platter	*jùng sìk pīng póon*	中式拼盤
cold dishes	*lăang chōi*	冷菜

cold hors d'oeuvre	*lǎang póon*	冷盤
combination platter	*pīng póon*	拼盤
fruit salad	*jǎap gwóh sà lūt*	雜果沙律
hot dishes	*yīt fàn*	熱葷
hot entrées	*tau póon*	頭盤
Japanese combination platter	*yǎt sìk pīng póon*	日式拼盤
jellyfish and hocks	*hói jīt fàn tai*	海蜇醮蹄
roast meat combination platter	*sìu méi pīng póon*	燒味拼盤
salad	*sà lūt*	沙律
salad with lobster	*lung hà sà lūt*	龍蝦沙律
salad with prawns	*dāai hà sà lūt*	大蝦沙律
salmon	*sàam man yúe*	三文魚
seafood combination platter	*hói sìn pīng póon*	海鮮拼盤
suckling pig combination platter	*yǔe jùe pīng póon*	乳豬拼盤
vegetable salad	*jǎap chōi sà lūt*	雜菜沙律

Main Dishes

The Cantonese are known for their ability to eat *anything*. It's said that the only four-legged thing they won't eat is a table, and the only thing that flies that they won't eat is an aeroplane!

I would like to order ... and ...
  m gói, ngóh séung gīu dì ... tung   唔該,我想叫...同埋...
  maai ...

Meat & Poultry

bacon	*yìn yūk*	煙肉
barbecue pork	*chà sìu*	叉燒
beef	*ngau yūk*	牛肉
beef ball	*ngau yūk yúen*	牛肉丸
chicken	*gài yūk*	雞肉
Chinese sausage	*lãap chéung*	臘腸
crispy pork	*sìu yūk*	燒肉
dried fluffy meat	*yūk sùng*	肉鬆
duck	*ngāap yuk*	鴨肉
ham	*fóh túi*	火腿
meat	*yūk*	肉
meat ball	*yūk yúen*	肉丸
minced beef	*mǐn jī ngau yūk*	免治牛肉
mutton	*yeung yūk*	羊肉
Peking duck	*bàk gìng tin ngāap*	北京塡鴨
pigeon	*bāak gāp*	白鴿
pork	*jùe yūk*	豬肉
quail	*ngàm chùn*	鵪鶉
roast duck	*sìu ngāap*	燒鴨
roast goose	*sìu ngóh*	燒鵝
roast suckling pig	*sìu yǔe jùe*	燒乳豬
sausage	*hèung chéung*	香腸
shrimp	*hà*	蝦
spare rib	*paai gwàt*	排骨
turkey	*fóh gài*	火雞
wild animal meat	*yě méi*	野味

Seafood

The most important part of the Cantonese cuisine is fresh seafood. Unlike other cuisines, all ingredients in Cantonese dishes keep their original flavour. Merely from tasting, it's possible to know which fish was used, or even how fresh the catch was, or whether it has been frozen. The best place to taste fresh seafood is in a floating restaurant.

Most, if not all, seafood restaurants keep tanks on their premises so that the seafood is as fresh as possible.

abalone	*bàau yue*	鮑魚
barramundi	*lǒ súe bàan*	老鼠斑
carp	*léi yúe*	鯉魚
clam	*pőng*	蚌
crab	*hǎai*	蟹
crabmeat (minced)	*hǎai fán*	蟹粉
crab roe	*hǎai wong*	蟹黃
crayfish	*lung hà*	龍蝦
cuttlefish	*mǎk yue*	墨魚
dace	*leng yúe*	鯪魚
dried scallop	*gòn yiu chǔe*	干瑤柱
eel	*maan*	鰻
fish	*yúe*	魚
fishball	*yue dāan*	魚蛋
fish maw (bladder)	*yue tő*	魚肚
fish meat	*yue yūk*	魚肉
garoupa	*sěk bàan*	石斑
jellyfish	*hói jīt*	海蜇
lobster	*lung hà*	龍蝦
mullet	*wòo táu*	烏頭
mussel	*chèng háu*	青口
octopus	*bāat jáau yue*	八爪魚
oyster	*ho*	蠔

perch	*lo yúe*	鱸魚
prawn	*dāai hà*	大蝦
raw fish	*yue sàang*	魚生
salmon	*sàam man yúe*	三文魚
salted fish	*haam yúe*	鹹魚
scallop	*dāai jí*	帶子
sea cucumber	*hói sàm*	海參
seafood	*hói sìn*	海鮮
sea snails	*héung lóh*	响螺
shad	*si yúe*	鰣魚
Shanghai crab	*dāai jǎap hǎai*	大閘蟹
shark's fin	*yue chī*	魚翅
shellfish	*lóh*	螺
shrimp	*hà*	蝦
shrimp ball	*hà yúen*	蝦丸
sole	*tāat sà*	撻沙
squid	*yau yúe*	魷魚
trout	*jùn yúe*	鱒魚
tuna	*gàm chèung yúe*	金鎗魚
white pomfret	*bǎak chòng yúe*	白鯧魚

Vegetables, Nuts, etc

asparagus	*lõ sún*	露筍
bamboo shoots	*jùk sún*	竹筍
beancurd (tofu)	*dǎu fõo*	豆腐
beans	*dǎu gōk*	豆角
bean sprouts	*nga chōi*	芽菜
bitter melon	*fóo gwà*	苦瓜
broccoli	*sài laan fà*	西蘭花
cabbage	*ye chōi*	椰菜
capsicum	*chèng jìu*	青椒

carrot	*hung loh bǎak*	紅蘿蔔
cashew nut	*yìu gwóh*	腰果
cauliflower	*ye chōi fà*	椰菜花
celery	*sài kán*	西芹
Chinese cabbage	*bǎak chōi*	白菜
Chinese kale	*gāai láan*	芥蘭
Chinese leek	*gáu chōi*	韮菜
choko	*fǎt sáu gwà*	佛手瓜
corn	*sùk mǎi*	粟米
cucumber	*chèng gwà*	青瓜
dried vegetables	*chōi gòn*	菜干
eggplant	*ngái gwà*	矮瓜
flowering cabbage	*chōi sàm*	菜心
gourd	*sì gwà*	絲瓜
leek	*dǎai chùng*	大蔥
leek (yellowish)	*gáu wong*	韮黄
lettuce	*sàang chōi*	生菜
lotus root	*lin ngǎu*	蓮藕
lotus seed	*lin jí*	蓮子
melon	*gwà*	瓜
mushroom	*moh gòo*	磨菇
olive	*gāam lǎam*	橄欖
peanuts	*fà sàng*	花生
peas	*dáu*	豆
pea sprouts	*dǎu miu*	豆苗
pinenut	*chung jí*	松子
potato	*sue jái*	薯仔
pumpkin	*naam gwà*	南瓜
salted vegetables	*haam chōi*	鹹菜
seaweed	*jí chōi*	紫菜
shallot	*sūen*	蒜

snow peas	*hoh làan dáu*	荷蘭豆
spinach	*bòh chōi*	菠菜
spring onion	*chùng*	蔥
sweet potato	*fàan súe*	番薯
taro	*wŏo táu*	芋頭
tofu (beancurd)	*dãu fŏo*	豆腐
tomato	*fàan ké*	番茄
turnip	*loh bǎak*	蘿蔔
vegetable	*sòh chōi*	蔬菜
watercress	*sài yeung chōi*	西洋菜
wax gourd	*dùng gwà*	冬瓜

Fruit, Nuts & Sweet Food

apple	*ping gwóh*	蘋果
apricot	*hǎng*	杏
avocado	*ngau yau gwóh*	牛油果
banana	*hèung jìu*	香蕉
cherries	*chè lei jí*	車厘子
chestnuts	*lũt jí*	栗子
Chinese peach	*súi mãt to*	水蜜桃
Chinese plum	*móoi*	梅
coconut	*ye jí*	椰子
dates	*jó*	棗
dried fruit	*gòn gwóh*	干果
durian	*lau lin*	榴蓮
fig	*mo fà gwóh*	無花果
fresh fruit	*sàn sìn súi gwóh*	新鮮水果
fruit	*sàang gwóh*	生果
grapefruit	*sài yáu*	西柚
grapes	*tai jí*	提子
guava	*fàan sĕk láu*	番石榴

Hami melon	*hà mãt gwà*	哈蜜瓜
honeydew melon	*mãt gwà*	蜜瓜
jackfruit	*dãai sũe bòh loh*	大樹菠蘿
Japanese nashi pear	*súi jìng léĩ*	水晶梨
juice	*gwóh jàp*	果汁
kiwifruit	*kei yĩ gwóh*	奇異果
lemon	*ning mùng*	檸檬
lime	*chèng ning mùng*	青檸檬
longan (similar to lychee)	*lung ngãn*	龍眼
loquat	*pei pa*	枇杷
lychee	*lãi jì*	荔枝
mandarin	*gàm*	柑
mango	*mòng gwóh*	芒果
melon	*gwà*	瓜
mixed fruit platter	*sàang gwóh pĩng póon*	生果拼盤
nectarine	*yau tó*	油桃
nuts	*gwóh yan*	果仁
olive	*gāam lãam*	橄欖
orange	*cháang*	橙
pawpaw (papaya)	*mũk gwà*	木瓜
peach	*tó*	桃
peanut	*fà sàng*	花生
pear	*bè léĩ*	啤梨
persimmon	*chí*	柿
pineapple	*bòh loh*	菠蘿
plum	*léĩ*	李
pomegranate	*sēk láu*	石榴
pomelo	*yáu*	柚

raisins	*po to gòng*	葡萄干
star apple	*yeung tó*	楊桃
strawberries	*sī dòh bè léi*	士多啤厘
sugar cane	*gàm jē*	甘蔗
tangerine	*gàm*	柑
walnut	*hăp to*	合桃
water chestnut	*mă tái*	馬蹄
watermelon	*sài gwà*	西瓜

Dairy Products

butter	*ngau yau*	牛油
cheese	*jì sí*	芝士
cream	*năai yau*	奶油
evaporated milk	*fà năai*	花奶
ice cream	*sūet gò*	雪糕
margarine	*jĭk măt yau*	植物油
milk	*ngau năai*	牛奶
milk powder	*năai fán*	奶粉
skim milk	*tūet jì năai*	脫脂奶
sweet condensed milk	*tim lĭn năai*	甜鍊奶
yoghurt	*sùen năai*	酸奶

Condiments

barbecue sauce	*sìu hàau jēung*	燒烤醬
bean sauce	*mĭn sí jēung*	麵豉醬
black bean	*dāu sī*	豆豉
chicken essence	*gài jìng*	雞精
chilli	*lăat jìu*	辣椒
chilli sauce	*lăat jìu jēung*	辣椒醬
cinnamon	*yŭk gwāi*	肉桂

cloves	*dìng hèung*	丁香
coriander	*yuen sài*	芫茜
curry	*gā lèi*	咖喱
dark soy sauce	*lŏ chàu*	老抽
fish soy	*yue lŏ*	魚露
five-spices powder	*ng̃ hèung fán*	五香粉
garlic	*sūen tau*	蒜頭
ginger	*gèung*	薑
Hoisin sauce	*hói sìn jēung*	海鮮醬
honey	*măt tong*	蜜糖
horseradish, green (wasabi)	*yăt bóon gāai lăat*	日本芥辣
malt sugar	*măk nga tóng*	麥芽糖
mint	*bŏk hoh*	薄荷
MSG	*mēi jìng*	味精
mustard	*gáai lăat*	芥辣
mustard sauce	*gáai jēung*	芥醬
nutmeg	*dău kāu*	荳蔻
oil	*yau*	油
onion	*yeung chùng*	洋蔥
oyster sauce	*ho yau*	蠔油
paprika	*hung lăat jìu*	紅辣椒
parsley	*hèung chōi*	香菜
pepper	*woo jìu*	胡椒
peppered-salt	*jìu yim*	椒鹽
plum sauce	*mooi jí jēung*	梅子醬
red vinegar	*jìt chō*	浙醋
salt	*yim*	鹽
satay	*sā dè*	沙茶
sesame oil	*ma yau*	麻油
soy sauce	*sĭ yau*	豉油

spring onion	*chùng*	蔥
star aniseed	*bāat gōk*	八角
sugar	*tong*	糖
sweet sauce	*tim jēung*	甜醬
sweet savoury sauce	*jā jēung*	炸醬
tomato sauce	*ké jàp*	茄汁
vinegar	*chō*	醋
wasabi	*yắt bóon gāai lắat*	日本芥辣
wild pepper	*fà jìu*	花椒

Other Miscellaneous Foods

agar-agar jelly	*leung fán*	涼粉
baby food	*yìng yi sĭk bán*	嬰兒食品
bean vermicelli	*fán sì*	粉絲
congee (rice porridge)	*jùk*	粥
egg	*dáan*	蛋
flour	*mĭn fán*	麵粉
hot dog	*yĭt gáu*	熱狗
Japanese udon (thick noodles)	*wòo dùng*	烏多

Cooking Methods

bake by slow fire	*wòoi*	煨
baked	*gūk*	焗
barbecue	*sìu hàau*	燒烤
boil	*gwán*	滾
braised	*pa*	扒
brine	*yīp*	醃

broil	*chēuk*	灼
cook	*júe*	煮
deep-fried	*jā*	炸
dry-fried	*gòn sìu*	干燒
fried	*jìn*	煎
grilled	*sìu*	燒
pan-fried	*jìn*	煎
quick-fried	*bāau*	爆
roasted	*hàau*	烤
simmer	*màn*	炆
smoked	*fàn*	燻
steam boat	*dá bìn lo*	打邊爐
steam in close vessel	*dūn*	燉
steamed	*jìng*	蒸
stew	*hung sìu*	紅燒
stir-fried	*cháau*	炒
stir mix	*leung bŏon*	涼拌
teppanyaki	*tīt báan sìu*	鐵板燒

Beverages
Soft Drinks

apple juice	*ping gwóh jàp*	萍果汁
bean soya	*dāu năai* or	豆奶
	dāu jèung	豆漿
beverage	*yám bán*	飲品
chocolate milk	*jùe gòo lìk năai*	朱古力奶
chocolate milkshake	*jùe gòo lìk năai sìk*	朱古力奶昔
Coca Cola	*hóh háu hóh lŏk*	可口可樂
coconut juice	*ye jàp*	椰汁

coke	hóh lŏk	可樂
cold water	dūng súi	凍水
fizzy drink	hēi súi	汽水
fresh juice	sìn gwóh jàp	鮮果汁
fruit juice	gwóh jàp	果汁
ginger beer	gèung bè	薑啤
grapefruit juice	sài yáu jàp	西柚汁
iced coffee	dūng gā fè	凍咖啡
iced lemon tea	dūng ning mùng cha	凍檸檬茶
iced water	bìng súi	冰水
juice	gwóh jàp	果汁
lemonade	ning mùng hēi súi	檸檬汽水
milk	ngau năai	牛奶
milkshake	năai sìk	奶昔
mineral water	kwōng chuen súi	礦泉水
orange juice	cháang jàp	橙汁
pineapple juice	bòh loh jàp	菠蘿汁
Seven Up	chàt héi	七喜
soda water	sòh dá súi	梳打水
soft drink	hēi súi	汽水
sugar cane juice	jē jàp	蔗汁
tomato juice	fàan ké jàp	番茄汁
tonic	tòng lĭk	湯力
water	súi	水

Alcoholic Drinks

beer	bè jáu	啤酒
brandy	bāt làan déi	拔蘭地
champagne	hèung bàn	香檳
Chinese wine	jùng gwōk jáu	中國酒
draught beer	sàang bè	生啤

gin	jìn jáu	毡酒
Japanese rice wine (saké)	yãt bóon jáu	日本酒
red wine	hung jáu	紅酒
spirits	jáu	酒
whisky	wài sī géi	威士忌
white wine	bãak jáu	白酒
wine	po to jáu	葡萄酒

Hot Drinks

almond milk	hãng yan cha	杏仁茶
black coffee	jàai fè	齋啡
boiling water	gwán súi	滾水
camomile tea	gùk fà cha	菊花茶
Chinese herbal tea	leung cha	涼茶
Chinese tea	jùng gwōk cha	中國茶
coffee	gā fè	咖啡
green tea	lūk cha	綠茶
Horlicks	hó lãap hàk	好立克
hot chocolate	jùe gòo lìk	朱古力
hot fresh milk	yĩt sìn nãai	熱鮮奶
hot Shaoxing wine	sīu hīng jáu	紹興酒
jasmine tea	fà cha or	花茶
	hèung pín cha	香片茶
lemon tea	ning mùng cha	檸檬茶
milk	ngau nãai	牛奶
Ovaltine	òh wa tin	柯華田
Puer tea	pó léi cha	普洱茶
Puer and camomile	gùk pó	菊普
soya bean milk	dãu jèung	豆漿
sweet herb tea	ng̃ fà cha	五花茶

tea	*cha*	茶
tea with milk	*năi cha*	奶茶
Tieguanyin tea	*tīt gwòon yàm cha*	鐵觀音茶
Wulong tea	*wòo lúng cha*	烏龍茶

Soups

There are endless varieties of Cantonese tonic soups, too many to name in the following list. They are good for your health, although to first-timers and especially foreigners, some may taste odd.

Soup is usually served before the meal, but it can also be served during the meal.

asparagus soup	*lò sún tòng*	露筍湯
beancurd claypot	*dău fòo bò*	豆腐煲
broth	*shĕung tòng*	上湯
chicken soup	*gài tòng*	雞湯
chicken and shark's fin soup	*gài bàau chī tòng*	雞鮑翅湯
Chinese dried mushroom soup	*dùng gòo tòng*	冬菇湯
Ching-bo-leung tonic soup	*chìng bó léung*	清補涼
combination beancurd soup	*bāat jàn dău fòo gàng*	八珍豆腐羹
consommé	*chìng tòng*	清湯
corn soup	*sùk măi gàng*	粟米羹
corn soup with chicken	*gài yung sùk măi gàng*	雞蓉粟米羹
corn soup with crab meat	*hăai yŭk sùk măi gàng*	蟹肉粟米羹
cream soup	*gĕi lím tòng*	忌廉湯

dried scallop soup	*yiu chǘe gàng*	瑤柱羹
duckling soup	*ngāap sì gàng*	鴨絲羹
egg-drop soup	*dāan fà tòng*	蛋花湯
fish soup	*yúe tòng*	魚湯
ginseng soup	*yan sàm tòng*	人參湯
green pea soup	*chèng dáu tòng*	青豆湯
hot and sour soup	*sùen lāat tòng*	酸辣湯
Japanese miso soup	*yāt bóon mǐn sí tòng*	日本麵豉湯
Japanese osuimono (consommé)	*yāt bóon chìng tòng*	日本清湯
lobster soup	*lung hà tòng*	龍蝦湯
lotus root soup	*lin ngǎu tòng*	蓮藕湯
mushroom soup	*moh gòo tòng*	磨菇湯
onion soup	*yeung chùng tòng*	洋蔥湯
oxtail soup	*ngau měi tòng*	牛尾湯
Russian broth	*loh sūng tòng*	羅宋湯
seafood soup	*hói sìn tòng*	海鮮湯
shark's fin soup	*yue chī gàng*	魚翅羹
snake gravy soup	*se gàng*	蛇羹
soup	*tòng*	湯
soup of the day	*lāi tòng*	例湯
steam boat	*dá bìn lo*	打邊爐
tomato soup	*fàan ké tòng*	番茄湯
vegetable soup	*jǎap chōi tòng*	雜菜湯
whole wax gourd soup	*dùng gwà jùng*	多瓜盅

Some Useful Words
Cutlery & Accessories

ashtray	*yìn fòoi gòng*	煙灰缸
basket	*lung*	籠
bottle	*jùn*	樽
bowl	*wóon*	碗
box	*hǎp*	盒
can	*gwōon*	罐
chair	*dāng*	櫈
chopsticks	*fāai jí*	筷子
cup	*bòoi*	杯
fork	*chà*	叉
knife and fork	*dò chà*	刀叉
knife	*dò*	刀
napkin	*jí gàn*	紙巾
packet	*bàau*	包
plate	*dīp*	碟
pot	*woo*	壺
rice bowl	*fāan wóon*	飯碗
scoop (for rice)	*faan hōk*	飯殼
scoop (for soup)	*tòng gàng*	湯羹
spoon	*chi gàng*	匙羹
table	*tói*	枱
tablecloth	*tói bō*	枱布
teapot	*cha wóo*	茶壺
teaspoon	*cha gàng*	茶羹
toothpick	*nga chìm*	牙簽
tray	*poon*	盤
wet towel	*sàp mo gàn*	濕毛巾
wine glass	*jáu bòoi*	酒杯

Others

10% service charge	*gà yàt síu jēung*	加一小賬
bill	*dàan*	單
chef	*dāai chúe*	大廚
delicious	*hó sĭk*	好食
fresh	*sàn sìn*	新鮮
full house	*mŏon jŏh*	滿座
manager	*gìng léi*	經理
service charge	*fŭk mŏ fāi*	服務費
share table	*dāap tói*	搭枱
smells nice	*hó hèung*	好香
the bill, please	*maai dàan*	埋單
tips	*tìp sí*	貼士
toilet	*sái sáu gàan*	洗手間
VIP	*gwāi bàn*	貴賓
waiter (f)	*síu jé*	小姐
waiter (m)	*fóh gēi*	伙記

Fruit

Shopping

Hong Kong is great for shopping. There's a huge variety of goods available, and best of all, there are no import duties for most merchandise. The period between December and the Chinese New Year is the best time for shopping around in Hong Kong. To avoid counterfeits, factory rejects and defective equipment in Hong Kong, shop in HKTA-recommended shops, or those offering international guarantees.

Macau is similar to Hong Kong although the range is smaller. Even liquor and tobacco are without import duties in Macau.

In China there is a limited range of imported goods but the shops are full of traditional Chinese artifacts. China is the mother country of tea, silk products and chinaware; and is still the world leader in these fields. From the Friendship Stores and government department stores you can get guaranteed and good quality goods.

The 'free markets' around every corner of the cities in China attract many people, and they have reasonable quality goods at low prices. The street markets in Hong Kong sell *anything* and are worth visiting just for the experience.

I'd like to buy...
 ngőh séung mǎai ...   我想買...
I'm just looking around.
 ngőh sìn tái yàt tái   我先睇一睇
How much does this/that cost?
 nì/góh gōh géi dòh chín ā?   呢/嗰個幾多錢呀?
That is very expensive.
 gā chín hó gwāi   價錢好貴

That is cheap.
gā chin hó peng　　　價錢好平

Where can I buy a ...?
hái bīn dŏ hóh yĭ mǎai dó ...　　嗱邊度可以買到...?

Where is the nearest ...?
jūi kán gē ... hái bīn dŏ ā?　　最近嘅...喺邊度呀?

I am looking for a ... .
ngŏh wán gán ...　　我搵緊...

7-Eleven store	*chàt săp yàt bĭn lĕi dīm*	七/十一便利店
antique shop	*góo wóon dīm*	古玩店
baker	*mĭn bàau pó*	麵飽舖
bank	*ngan hong*	銀行
barber	*fèi fāat pó*	飛髮舖
bookshop	*sùe gúk*	書局
butcher	*yŭk pó*	肉舖
camera shop	*sīp yíng hēi choi gùng sì*	攝影器材公司
Chinese product emporium	*jùng gwōk gwōk fōh gùng sì*	中國國貨公司
department store	*bāak fōh gùng sì*	百貨公司
dress shop	*sing yì dīm*	成衣店
duty free shop	*mĭn sūi dīm*	免稅店
electrical shop	*dĭn hēi pó*	電器舖
florist	*fà dīm*	花店
free market	*jĭ yau sĭ cheung*	自由市場
Friendship store	*yău yi sèung dīm*	友誼商店
fruit shop	*sàang gwóh pó*	生果舖
goldsmith	*gàm pó*	金舖
grocery	*jăap fōh pó*	雜貨舖

hairdresser	*fāat long*	髮廊
handicraft shop	*gùng ngãi bán dīm*	工藝品店
jade free market	*yūk hēi sí cheung*	玉器市場
Japanese department store	*yàt bóon bāak fōh gùng sì*	日本百貨公司
jeweller's shop	*jùe bó hóng*	珠寶行
ladies' free market	*nũi yán gàai*	女人街
laundry	*sái yì pó*	洗衣舖
lunar New Year's Eve free market	*nin sìu sí cheung*	年宵市場
market	*sí cheung*	市場
money exchange	*jáau wõon dīm*	找換店
musical instrument shop	*ngõk hēi hóng*	樂器行
pharmacy	*yẽuk fong*	藥房
shoe shop	*haai pó*	鞋舖
shop	*pō táu*	舖頭
shopping arcade	*sèung cheung*	商場
shopping centre	*kāu mãt jùng sàm*	購物中心
souvenir shop	*lái bán dīm*	禮品店
stall	*dōng*	檔
store	*sī dòh*	士多
supermarket	*chìu kàp sí cheung*	超級市場
tailor	*choi fúng dīm*	裁縫店
trading firm	*sèung hóng*	商行
vegetable shop	*chōi pó*	菜舖

Bargaining

Bargaining is an art. Some people do bargain while others don't, but you may ask if you could negotiate prices: *yáu mõ gā góng ā?* Normally, at privately owned shops or stalls, you stand a better chance of bargaining than at the government-owned ones. Also, buying more will increase your negotiating power. But before doing so, make sure you have the things you want, and don't bother buying poor quality goods, even if they are cheap.

You may also express the amount you wish to pay for the goods by keying the figure in a calculator and showing it to the vendor. It's also advisable to check other prices before buying.

Department stores are unlikely to be good places for bargaining; like anywhere, the ideal time for bargains is during their occasional sales.

It's too expensive.
   tāai gwāi lā   太貴啦

Can you reduce the price?
   peng dì dàk m dàk ā?   平啲得唔得呀?

Do you give a discount?
   yáu mő jīt tau dá ā?   有冇折頭打呀?

Can you give a 20% discount?
   dá gōh bāat jīt dàk m dàk ā?   打個八折得唔得呀?

bargaining	*góng gā*	講價
discount	*jīt kāu*	折扣
half price	*bōon gā*	半價
no bargain	*mő gā góng*	冇價講
no second price	*bàt yĭ gā*	不二價
on sale	*dãai gáam gā*	大減價
sale	*dãai peng mãai*	大平賣
sold out	*mãai sāai*	賣晒

Souvenirs

calligraphy	*sùe fàat*	書法
carpets	*dēi jìn*	地氈
chinaware	*chi hēi*	瓷器
chopsticks	*fāai jí*	筷子
curios	*góo wóon*	古玩
dolls	*gùng jái*	公仔
earrings	*yí wáan*	耳環
embroidery	*chī sāu*	刺繡
fabrics	*bō lĭu*	布料
fans	*sīn*	扇
foods	*sĭk bán*	食品
furniture	*gà sì*	傢俬
gold products	*gàm hēi*	金器
handbag	*sáu dói*	手袋
handicrafts	*sáu gùng ngǎi bán*	手工藝品
jade products	*yŭk hēi*	玉器
jewellery	*jùe bó*	珠寶
lacquerware	*chàt hēi*	漆器
leatherwork	*pei gŭi*	皮具
musical instruments	*ngōk hēi*	樂器
necklace	*géng lín*	頸鍊
paintings	*wá*	畫
paper cuts	*jín jí*	剪紙
pearl	*jàn jùe*	珍珠
personal seal	*to jèung*	圖章
porcelain	*chi hēi*	瓷器
postcard	*ming sūn pín*	明信片
pottery	*to hēi*	陶器

scrolls	*gúen jūk*	卷軸
sculpture	*dìu hàk*	雕刻
shuttlecock	*yín*	毽
silk products	*sì jìk*	絲織
silver products	*ngan hēi*	銀器
souvenirs	*gēi nĭm bán*	記念品
toys	*wŏon gŭi*	玩具

Audio/Video & Photography

Hong Kong has one of the best audio/video markets in the world, where you can find the latest and most advanced models of almost any product at a reasonable price.

amplifier	*kwōng yàm gèi*	擴音機
audio/video shop	*yàm héung hēi choi dīm*	音響器材店
automatic camera	*chuen jī dūng yíng séung gèi*	全自動影相機
B&W film	*hàk bāak fèi lám*	黑白菲林
camera	*séung gèi*	相機
cassette tape	*kà sìk lūk yàm dáai*	卡式錄音帶
cassette tape recorder	*kà sìk lūk yàm gèi*	卡式錄音機
CD	*CD sāi díp*	ＣＤ細碟
colour	*chói sìk*	彩色
colour film	*chói sìk fèi lám*	彩色菲林
colour slide	*chói sìk wăan dàng pín*	彩色幻燈片
eight mm video tape	*bāat mǎi lei lūk yíng dáai*	八米厘錄影帶

film	*fèi lám*	菲林
flash	*sím gwòng dàng*	閃光燈
Fuji film	*fōo sī fèi lám*	富士菲林
instant camera	*jìk yíng jìk yáu séung gèi*	即影即有相機
Kodak film	*òh dǎat fèi lám*	柯達菲林
lens	*gēng tau*	鏡頭
lens cap	*séung gèi gōi*	相機蓋
lens paper (cleaning tissue)	*māat gēng tau jí*	抹鏡頭紙
light meter	*chàk gwòng bìu*	測光表
NTSC system	*NTSC sīn lǒ*	NTSC線路
microphone	*mài gò fùng*	咪高峰
overhead projector	*gò yíng gèi*	高影機
PAL system	*PAL sīn lǒ*	PAL線路
photo	*sēung pín*	相片
radio	*sàu yàm gèi*	收音機
record	*chéung pín*	唱片
recorder	*lūk yàm gèi*	錄音機
slide projector	*wǎan dàng gèi*	幻燈機
timer	*si gāan jāi*	時間掣
tripod	*sàam gēuk gá*	三腳架
TV	*dīn sī*	電視
video camera	*sīp lūk gèi*	攝錄機
video laser disc	*lui sě yíng díp*	雷射影碟
video tape	*lūk yíng dáai*	錄影帶
waterproof	*fong súi*	防水
wide angle lens	*gwóng gōk gēng*	廣角鏡
zoom lens	*san gēng*	神鏡

Computers

computer	*dīn nőu*	電腦
computer shop	*dīn nőu gùng sì*	電腦公司
floppy disc	*chi díp*	磁碟
hardware	*ngǎang gín*	硬件
software	*yűen gín*	軟件
virus	*běng dũk*	病毒

Duty Free Shopping

Hong Kong established the first modern duty free shop straight after the Korean War. Nowadays, they supply not only the duty-exempted liquor and tobacco but also all the usual imported perfumes, and so on.

a bottle of	*yàt jùn*	一樽
a box	*yàt hǎp*	一盒
a carton of cigarettes	*yàt tiu yìn*	一條煙
imported liquor	*yeung jáu*	洋酒
liquor	*līt jáu*	烈酒
ounce	*ngòn sí*	安士
perfume	*hèung súi*	香水
tobacco	*yìn sì*	煙絲
watch	*sáu bìu*	手錶

Clothing

Imported and locally made fashions for both men and women are abundant in Hong Kong and can be bought at realistic prices, especially at the markets. Tailors exist in profusion as made-to-measure is popular and relatively cheap.

belt	*pei dáai*	皮帶
blouse	*nűi jòng sēung yì*	女裝上衣
boot	*cheung hèuh*	長靴
casual dress	*bīn jòng*	便裝
clothing	*yì fūk*	衣服
coat	*ngŏi tō*	外套
dress	*tō jòng*	套裝
formal dress	*lăi fūk*	禮服
gloves	*sáu tō*	手套
handerchief	*sáu gàn*	手巾
hat	*mó*	帽
jacket	*sēung yì*	上衣
jacket (traditional)	*jùng sàan jòng*	中山裝
jeans	*ngau jái fōo*	牛仔褲
jumper	*yeung mo làang sàam*	羊毛冷衫
long gown (Manchu woman's)	*kei pó*	旗袍
long sleeves	*cheung jău*	長袖
man's long gown (traditional)	*cheung sàm*	長衫
pants	*dúen fōo*	短褲
raincoat	*yűe yì*	雨衣
sandals	*leung haai*	涼鞋
shirt	*sùt sàam*	袖衫
shoes	*haai*	鞋
shorts	*dúen fōo*	短褲
skirt	*kwan*	裙
socks	*mắt*	襪
suit	*sài jòng*	西裝
sweater	*yeung mo sàam*	羊毛衫

swimming suit	*yau wǐng yì*	游泳衣
tie	*tàai*	呔
trousers	*fōo*	褲
T-shirt	*T-sùt*	T-裇
underwear	*nǒi yì*	內衣
uniform	*jāi fūk*	制服
Western-style suit	*sài jòng*	西裝

Materials

cashmere	*kè sī mè*	茄士咩
cotton	*min*	棉
leather	*péi*	皮
linen	*ma*	麻
satin	*dūen*	緞
silk	*sì*	絲
wool	*mo*	毛

Colours

Traditionally, red was, and probably still is, the most popular colour for the Chinese when celebrating a joyous occasion such as a wedding or birthday, and it's popular for decorations for the new year. White is the colour used to mark a sad or mournful occasion, such as a funeral.

dark ...	*sàm ...*	深...
light ...	*chín ...*	淺...
black	*hàk*	黑
blue	*laam*	藍
brown	*fè*	啡
golden	*gàm*	金
green	*lūk*	綠

grey	*fòoi*	灰
orange	*cháang*	橙
pink	*fán hung*	粉紅
red	*hung*	紅
silver	*ngan*	銀
violet	*jí*	紫
white	*bǎak*	白
yellow	*wong*	黃

Descriptions

big	*dǎai*	大
cheap	*peng*	平
expensive	*gwāi*	貴
fit	*ngàam*	啱
handmade	*sáu gùng jǒ*	手工造
long	*cheung*	長
loose	*fōot*	闊
pretty	*lēng*	靚
short	*dúen*	短
small	*sāi*	細
tight	*gán*	緊

Stationery & Publications

ballpoint pen	*yuen jí bàt*	原子筆
book	*sùe*	書
calculator	*gāi sǒ gèi*	計數機
calendar	*yǎt lǐk*	日曆
calligraphic model	*jǐ típ*	字貼
clag	*jèung woo*	漿糊
correction fluid	*gói chōh súi*	改錯水

crayons	*lăap bàt*	蠟筆
dictionary	*jī dín*	字典
envelope	*sūn fùng*	信封
exercise book	*lĭn jăap bó*	練習部
file	*man gín gáap*	文件夾
ink	*măk súi*	墨水
ink stone	*măk yín*	墨硯
ink tablet	*măk*	墨
letter pad	*sūn jí*	信紙
magazine	*jăap jī*	雜誌
map	*dĕi to*	地圖
newspaper	*bō jí*	報紙
newspaper in English	*yìng mán bō jí*	英文報紙
novel	*síu sūet*	小說
paper	*jí*	紙
pencil	*yuen bàt*	鉛筆
scissors	*gāau jín*	較剪
stapler	*dèng sùe gèi*	釘書機
sticky tape	*gàau jí*	膠紙
typewriter	*dá jī gèi*	打字機
weekly magazine	*jàu hòn*	週刊
writing brush	*mo bàt*	毛筆

Toiletries

baby powder	*yìng yi sóng sàn fán*	嬰兒爽身粉
baby's bottle	*năai jùn*	奶樽
comb	*sòh*	梳
conditioner	*woo fàat sō*	護髮素
dental floss	*nga sīn*	牙線

deodorant	*chui chāu jài*	除臭劑
distilled water	*jìng lǎu súi*	蒸溜水
dummy	*nǎai júi*	奶咀
hairbrush	*sòh*	梳
hair cream	*fāat yǔe*	髮乳
moisturising cream	*yǔn fòo sèung*	潤膚霜
razor	*tāi dò*	剃刀
shampoo	*sái tau súi*	洗頭水
shaving cream	*tāi sò gò*	剃鬚膏
soap	*fàan gáan*	番梘
sunblock cream	*tāai yeung yau*	太陽油
talcum powder	*sóng sàn fán*	爽身粉
tissues	*jí gàn*	紙巾
toilet paper	*chī jí*	廁紙
toothbrush	*nga cháat*	牙刷
toothpaste	*nga gò*	牙膏
vaseline	*fà sī líng*	花士令

For more specific health needs, see At the Chemist on page 166.

Sizes & Quantities

10% discount	*gáu jīt*	九折
20% discount	*bāat jīt*	八折
a little bit	*yàt dì*	一啲
big	*dǎai*	大
bigger	*dǎai dì*	大啲
biggest	*jūi dǎai*	最大
enough	*gāu*	夠
heavy	*chǔng*	重
less	*síu dì*	少啲
light(weight)	*hèng*	輕

long	cheung	長
many	dòh	多
more	dòh di	多啲
none	mő	冇
short	dúen	短
small	sāi	細
smaller	sāi dì	細啲
smallest	jūi sāi	最細
tall	gò	高
the most ...	jūi ...	最...
too many/much	tāai dòh	太多

Some Useful Words

battery	dīn chi	電池
battery charger	chùng dīn hēi	充電器
brass	tung hēi	銅器
briefcase	gùng sī bàau	公事包
calculator	gāi sō gèi	計數機
copy machine	yíng yān gèi	影印機
discount	jīt tau, or jīt kāu	折頭/折扣
electrical cord	dīn sīn	電線
fax machine	chuen jàn gèi	傳眞機
invoice	fāat pīu	發票
microwave oven	mei bòh lo	微波爐
receipt	sàu gūi	收據

Health

In Hong Kong, it's quite easy to find a doctor any time from early morning till late evening; and there's always the emergency surgery in the public hospital. Usually patients can be supplied immediately with prescribed medicines by their doctors. Most doctors can speak English, but there are some local doctors who practise the traditional Chinese method of medicine and only communicate in their native tongues. Unlike the licensed doctors, these natural therapists prescribe mixtures of Chinese herbs, generally very strong and sometimes repulsive smelling, which can usually be bought right next door to the clinics.

In some bigger and more modern Cantonese cities in China, one can find a few doctors who speak English. But if you have to visit a doctor in a remote area, you'll need to take along an interpreter. You should also be prepared and carry a basic medical kit with any prescribed drugs you need.

I am sick.
ngőh yấu běng   我有病

My friend is sick.
ngőh pang yấu yấu běng   我朋友有病

I need a doctor.
ngőh yīu wán yì sàng   我要搵醫生

I need a doctor who can speak English.
ngőh yīu wán sìk góng yìng mán gē yì sàng   我要搵識講英文嘅醫生

Please call a doctor to room ...
chéng gīu yì sàng lai ... hő fóng   請叫醫生嚟 ... 號房

Please take me to a doctor.
chéng dāai ngőh hūi tái yì sàng 請帶我去睇醫生

I have been injured.
ngőh sǎu jóh sèung 我受咗傷

I need an ambulance.
ngőh yīu gīu gāu sèung chè 我要叫救傷車

I need first aid.
ngőh sùi yīu gàp gāu 我需要急救

Could you tell me where the ... is?	*chéng mǎn ... hái bìn dő ā?*	請問...喺邊度呀?
casualty ward (emergency department)	*gàp jīng sàt*	急症室
clinic	*chán sóh*	診所
doctor	*yì sàng*	醫生
hospital	*yì yúen*	醫院
nurse	*wőo sĩ*	護士
operating theatre	*sáu sũt sàt*	手術室
pharmacy	*yěuk fong*	藥房

At the Hospital/Clinic

I need an English interpreter.
ngőh yīu wán yàt wái yìng mán fàan yĩk 我要搵一位英文翻譯

I want a female doctor.
ngőh yīu wán yàt wái nűi yì sàng 我要搵一位女醫生

Please use a new syringe.
chéng yűng sàn gē jàm 請用新嘅針

I have my own syringe.
ngőh yắu jĩ géi ge jàm 我有自己嘅針

I don't want a blood transfusion.
ngőh m yīu sùe hūet　　　　　　　我唔要輸血

At the Doctor
I am not feeling well.
ngőh m sùe fūk　　　　　　　　　我唔舒服
How long before it will get better?
yīu géi női sìn jî hóh yî hó fàan?　　要幾耐先至可以好番?
I need a pregnancy test.
ngőh yīu yĭm yăn　　　　　　　　我要驗孕

Questions
What's wrong?
néî yău màt yé sî ā?　　　　　　　你有乜嘢事呀?
Where does it hurt?
néî bìn dő m sùe fūk ā?　　　　　你邊度唔舒服呀?
How are you feeling?
néî yi gà gōk dàk dím ā?　　　　　你而家覺得點呀?
Do you feel any pain?
tūng m tūng ā?　　　　　　　　　痛唔痛呀?
Do you have a temperature?
néî yău mő fāat sìu ā?　　　　　你有冇發燒呀?
What illness have you had in the past?
*néî yî chin yău gwōh màt yé
bèng ā?*　　　　　　　　　　　你以前有過乜嘢病呀?
Do you smoke?
néî ping si yău mő sĭk yìn ā?　　　你平時有冇食煙呀?
Do you drink?
néî ping si yău mő yám jáu ā?　　你平時有冇飲酒呀?
Are you pregnant?
hăi m hăi waai jóh yăn ā?　　　　係唔係懷咗孕呀?

Ailments

I am/feel/have ...	*ngőh ...*	我...
been bitten by an insect	*bĕi chung ngáau*	被蟲咬
can't move my ...	*gē ... m yùk dàk*	嘅...唔郁得
can't sleep	*fān m jĕuk*	瞓唔着
a heart condition	*yáu sàm jŏng bĕng*	有心臟病
loss of appetite	*sĭk jăi*	食滯
not had my period for ... months	*tìng jóh gìng ... gōh yŭet*	停咗經...個月
on the pill	*sĭk gán bĕi yān yúen*	食緊避孕丸
painful and sore all over	*yìu sùen gwàt tūng*	腰酸骨痛
palpitation/high pulse rate	*sàm tīu gàp chùk*	心跳急促
pregnant	*waai yán*	懷孕
a skin lesion	*pei fòo súen sèung*	皮膚損傷
thrown up, vomited	*ngáu tō*	嘔吐
very tired	*hó gwŏoi*	好攰
tired, no concentration	*mŏ jìng san*	冇精神
tired, no strength	*jàu sàn mŏ lĭk*	週身冇力
weak, lethargic	*sàn tái hùi yĕuk*	身體虛弱

It's ...	*nì dŏ ...*	呢度...
bleeding	*lau hūet*	流血
broken	*tŭen jóh*	斷咗
bruised	*yúe jóh*	瘀咗

dislocated	*làt jóh gāau*	甩咗骹
sprained	*náu sèung*	扭傷
swollen	*júng jóh*	腫咗

I have (a/an) ...	*ngóh ...*	我...
altitude sickness	*yáu wāi gò jīng*	有畏高症
appendicitis	*yáu maang chéung yìm*	有盲腸炎
arthritis	*yáu gwàan jīt yim*	有關節炎
asthma	*hàau chúen*	哮喘
backache	*yìu tūng*	腰痛
breathing trouble	*fòo kàp kwūn naan*	呼吸困難
breathless	*hēi chúen*	氣喘
burn	*bēi sìu sèung*	被燒傷
cold	*yáu sèung fùng*	有傷風
cold sweat	*chùt láang hōn*	出冷汗
constipated	*bīn bēi*	便秘
cough	*yáu kàt sāu*	有咳嗽
cramps	*chàu gàn*	抽筋
diabetes	*yáu tong nīu bēng*	有糖尿病
diarrhoea	*tó ngóh*	肚痾
dizzy	*tau wan*	頭暈
fever	*fāat sìu*	發燒
food poisoning	*sīk mát jūng dūk*	食物中毒
hay fever	*yáu fà fán gwōh mán jīng*	有花粉過敏症
headache	*tau tūng*	頭痛
hepatitis	*yáu gòn yim*	有肝炎
high blood pressure	*yáu gò hūet ngáat*	有高血壓
indigestion	*sìu fā bàt leung*	消化不良

influenza	yáu gám mõ	有感冒
insomnia	sàt min	失眠
itch	han yéung	痕癢
lice	yáu sāt	有虱
low blood pressure	yáu dài hūet ngāat	有低血壓
malaria	yáu yēuk jăt	有瘧疾
migraine	yáu pìn tau tūng	有偏頭痛
nervous breakdown	san gìng sùi yēuk	神經衰弱
neuralgia	san gìng tūng	神經痛
no appetite	mõ wãi háu	冇胃口
rheumatism	yáu fùng sàp	有風濕
seasickness	wan suen lõng	暈船浪
sore throat	hau lung tūng	喉嚨痛
stomachache	tõ tūng	肚痛
stomach ulcer	yáu wãi kóoi yeung	有胃潰瘍
sunstroke	jūng súe	中暑
tonsillitis	yáu bín to sīn yim	有扁桃腺炎
toothache	nga tūng	牙痛
travel sickness	wan lõng	暈浪
typhoid	yáu sèung hon	有傷寒
venereal disease	yáu sīng bēng	有性病

Allergies

I'm allergic to	ngõh dūi ... gwōh mán	我對...過敏
antibiotics	kōng sàng sō	抗生素
aspirin	ā sĩ pàt ling	亞士匹靈
codeine	hóh dõi yàn	可待因
dairy products	yũe lõk sĩk mãt	乳酪食物
food colouring	sĩk mãt sìk sō	食物色素

meat	*yŭk lūi sīk māt*	肉類食物
MSG	*mĕi jìng*	味精
oranges	*cháang*	橙
penicillin	*poon nei sài lam*	盤尼西林
pollen	*fà fán*	花粉

I have skin allergies.

    ngŏh yáu pei fòo mán gám   我有皮膚敏感

Parts of the Body

ankle	*gēuk ngăan*	腳眼
appendix	*maang chéung*	盲腸
arm	*sáu bēi*	手臂
back	*bōoi jēk*	背脊
beard	*woo sò*	鬍鬚
blood	*hūet*	血
bone	*gwàt*	骨
breast	*yŭe fong*	乳房
chest	*hùng bŏ*	胸部
ear	*yĭ*	耳
eye	*ngăan*	眼
face	*mĭn*	面
faeces	*dāai bīn*	大便
finger	*sáu jí*	手指
fingernail	*jí gàap*	指甲
foot	*gēuk*	腳
gall bladder	*dáam nong*	胆囊
gallstone	*dáam sĕk*	胆石
hair	*tau fāat*	頭髮
hand	*sáu*	手
head	*tau*	頭

heart	*sàm jŏng*	心臟
hip	*tuen bŏ*	臀部
kidney	*săn jŏng*	腎臟
leg	*dăai túi*	大腿
liver	*gòn jŏng*	肝臟
lung	*făi*	肺
mouth	*háu*	口
muscle	*gèi yūk*	肌肉
neck	*géng*	頸
nerve	*san gìng*	神經
nose	*bĕi*	鼻
pulse	*măk bŏk*	脈搏
shoulder	*bŏk tau*	膊頭
skin	*pei fòo*	皮膚
spine	*jēk jùi*	脊椎
stomach	*wăi*	胃
throat	*hau lung*	喉嚨

tonsils	*bín to sīn*	扁桃腺
urinate	*síu bǐn*	小便
urine	*nǐu*	尿

At the Chemist

When you visit a doctor, the prescribed medicine is usually provided. However there are some cases when the doctor is unable to do so. It is then up to you to acquire the prescription from a chemist. Make sure that you know the correct dosage.

May I have a/the ..., please?	*m gòi béi ngǒh ...*	唔該俾我...
antipyretic tablet	*tūi sìu yěuk*	退燒藥
aspirin	*ā sī pàt ling*	亞士匹靈
bandage	*sà bō*	紗布
Band-aids	*yěuk súi gàau bō*	藥水膠布
condom	*běi yǎn tō*	避孕套
cotton stick	*min pǎang*	棉棒
cough remedy	*jí kàt yěuk*	止咳藥
eye drops	*ngǎan yěuk súi*	眼藥水
insect repellent	*màn pā súi*	蚊怕水
iodine	*dìn jáu*	碘酒
laxative	*jí sē yěuk*	止瀉藥
mercurochrome	*hung yěuk súi*	紅藥水
painkiller	*jí tūng yěuk*	止痛藥
sanitary napkins	*wǎi sàng gàn*	衛生巾
sleeping pill	*ngòn min yěuk*	安眠藥
the pill (contraceptive)	*běi yǎn yúen*	避孕丸
thermometer	*tāam yīt jàm*	探熱針
Tiger balm	*mǎan gàm yau*	萬金油

tranquilliser	*jān jǐng jài*	鎮靜劑
travel sickness pill	*wan lõng yúen*	暈浪丸

Take (1) tablet each (4) times a day.
mõoi yãt (4) chī mõoi chi sĭk (1) làp 每日(4)次每次食(1)粒

Apply to the affected area (twice) a day.
mõoi yãt cha wǎan chūe (léung chī) 每日搽患處(兩次)

before/after meal
fāan chin/hǎu 飯前/後

before bedtime
lam fān chin 臨瞓前

At the Dentist

decayed tooth	*jūe nga*	蛀牙
dentist	*nga yì*	牙醫
denture	*gá nga*	假牙
filled teeth	*bó nga*	補牙
root of tooth	*nga gàn*	牙齦
teeth	*nga*	牙
tooth	*nga chí*	牙齒
toothache	*nga tūng*	牙痛
wisdom tooth	*jǐ wái chí*	智慧齒

Is there a dentist here?
chéng mǎn nì dõ yǎu mõ nga yì ā? 請問呢度有冇牙醫呀?

I don't want it extracted.
ngõh m yīu tūet nga 我唔要脫牙

Please give me an anaesthetic.
chéng yũng ma jūi yẽuk 請用麻醉藥

At the Optometrist

blind	*maang ngǎan*	盲眼
cataract	*bǎak nǒi jēung*	白內障
contact lens	*yán ying ngǎan géng*	隱形眼鏡
eye	*ngǎan jìng*	眼睛
eye drops	*ngǎan yěuk súi*	眼藥水
eye test	*yǐm ngǎan*	驗眼
glasses	*ngǎan géng*	眼鏡
long-sighted	*yúen sī*	遠視
optometrist	*yǐm ngǎan sì*	驗眼師
short-sighted	*gǎn sī*	近視

Some Useful Words

accident	*yī ngǒi*	意外
acupuncture	*jàm gāu*	針灸
AIDS	*ngòi jì běng* or	愛滋病
	ngǎai jì běng	艾滋病
antibiotic	*kōng sàng sō*	抗生素
antiseptic	*sìu dūk*	消毒
bandage	*sà bō*	紗布
bleed	*chùt hūet*	出血
blood group	*hūet ying*	血型
blood pressure	*hūet ngāat*	血壓
blood test	*yǐm hūet*	驗血
cancer	*ngaam*	癌
chronic	*mǎan sīng*	慢性
contraceptive	*běi yǎn yúen*	避孕丸
dispensary	*yěuk fong*	藥房
doctor	*yì sàng*	醫生
first aid	*gàp gāu*	急救

injection	*dá jàm*	打針
meningitis	*nó mõk yim*	腦膜炎
menstruation	*yũet gìng*	月經
nauseous	*jōk ngóu*	作嘔
physiotherapist	*māt léi jī liu sì*	物理治療師
pneumonia	*fāi yim*	肺炎
Red Cross	*hung sãp jī wóoi*	紅十字會
specialist	*jùen fòh yì sàng*	專科醫生
surgeon	*ngõi fòh yì sàng*	外科醫生
syringe	*jàm*	針
ultrasound	*chìu sìng bòh*	超聲波
virus	*bẽng dũk*	病毒
vitamin	*wai tà mĩng*	維他命
X-rays	*X gwòng*	X 光

People

Time, Dates & Festivals

Telling the Time

Telling the time in Cantonese is quite easy after you manage the numbers in the Numbers & Amounts chapter. Just try to remember a few key words:

hour	*jùng tau*	鐘頭
... o'clock	*... dím*	...點
half past ...	*... dím bōon*	...點半
minute	*fàn*	分
second	*míu*	秒

bāat dím
八點

sǎp dím yī sǎp fàn
十點二十分
10 o'clock 20 minutes

sǎp yàt dím sēi
sǎp ng̃ fàn
十一點四十五分
11 o'clock 40
+ 5 minutes

léung dím bōon or *léung dím sàam sǎp fàn*
兩點半   兩點三十分
2 o'clock half   2 o'clock 30 minutes

The common units for telling the time in Cantonese are *jī* (five minutes) and *gwàt* (a quarter).

a quarter (of an·hour)	*yàt gōh gwàt*	一個骨
a five-minute (sector of time)	*yàt gōh jī*	一個字

gáu dím ling n̄g fàn
九點零五分
9 o'clock + 5 minutes
or
gáu dím yàt gōh jī
九點一個字
9 o'clock a five-minute
(sector)

chàt dím sēi sāp n̄g fàn
七點四十五分
7 o'clock 40 + 5 minutes
or
chàt dím gáu gōh jī
七點九個字
7 o'clock 9 x a five-minute
(sector)
or
chàt dím sàam gōh gwàt
七點三個骨
7 o'clock 3 x quarter hours

If you want to specify the morning or afternoon, say the appropriate phrase before the time.

in the morning	*sēung ńg*	上午
in the afternoon	*hā ńg*	下午
noon	*jùng ńg*	中午
in the evening	*mǎan sēung*	晚上
midnight	*bōon yé*	半夜

sēung ńg chàt dím sǎp fàn
上午七點十分
7.10 am

mǎan sēung bāat dím bōon
晚上八點半
8.30 pm

hā ńg sàam dím sàam gōh jī
下午三點三個字
3.15 pm
in the afternoon 3 o'clock
3 x a five-minute (sector)

jùng ńg sǎp yī dím
中午十二點
noon 12 o'clock
or
bōon yé sǎp yī dím
半夜十二點
midnight

Days of the Week

Sunday	*sìng kei yāt*	星期日
Monday	*sìng kei yàt*	星期一
Tuesday	*sìng kei yī*	星期二
Wednesday	*sìng kei sàam*	星期三
Thursday	*sìng kei sēi*	星期四
Friday	*sìng kei ńg*	星期五
Saturday	*sìng kei lūk*	星期六
week	*sìng kei*	星期
this week	*gàm gōh sìng kei*	今個星期
last week	*sēung gōh sìng kei*	上個星期
next week	*hā gōh sìng kei*	下個星期
two weeks	*léung gōh sìng kei*	兩個星期
four weeks	*sēi gōh sìng kei*	四個星期

Days of the Month

Simply using the *yāt* or *hǒ* (colloquial) after the ordinal numbers.

... day	... *yāt*, or ... *hǒ*	...日，...號
the 1st day	*yàt yāt* or	一日
	yàt hǒ	一號
the 24th day	*yī sǎp sēi yāt* or	二十四日
	yī sǎp sēi hǒ	二十四號
today	*gàm yāt*	今日
yesterday	*kam yāt*	噙日
the day before yesterday	*chin yāt*	前日
two days before yesterday	*dāai chin yāt*	大前日
tomorrow	*tìng yāt*	聽日

the day after tomorrow	*hãu yãt*	後日
two days after tomorrow	*dãai hãu yãt*	大後日
tonight	*gàm màan*	今晚
last night	*kam mãan*	噚晚
tomorrow evening	*tìng màan*	聽晚

Months

January	*yàt yüet*	一月
February	*yĭ yüet*	二月
March	*sàam yüet*	三月
April	*sēi yüet*	四月
May	*nğ yüet*	五月
June	*lũk yüet*	六月
July	*chàt yüet*	七月
August	*bāat yüet*	八月
September	*gáu yüet*	九月
October	*sãp yüet*	十月
November	*sãp yàt yüet*	十一月
December	*sãp yĭ yüet*	十二月

January (lunar calendar)	*jìng yüet*	正月
leap year	*yün nin*	閏年
leap month (lunar calendar)	*yün yüet*	閏月
August (leap)	*yün bāat yüet*	閏八月
this month	*gàm gōh yüet*	今個月
last month	*sēung gōh yüet*	上個月
next month	*hã gōh yüet*	下個月

Seasons

spring	*chùn*	春
summer	*hā*	夏
autumn	*chàu*	秋
winter	*dùng*	冬
seasons	*gwāi jīt*	季節
rainy season	*yűe gwāi*	雨季

Dates

To express dates, the order is: year–month–day.

25 December
   sāp yī yűet yī sāp nğ yāt   十二月二十五日
   December 25 day

10 Feb 94
   gáu sēi nin yī yűet sāp yāt   九四年二月十日
   9 4 year February 10 day

Tuesday, 1 July, 1997
   yāt gáu gáu chàt nin chàt yűet yāt   一九九七年七月一
   yāt sìng kei yī   日星期二
   1 9 9 7 year July 1 day
   Tuesday

I was born in ... (year) ... (month) ...
   (day).
   ngőh hái ...nin ...yűet ...yāt chùt sāi   我喺...年...月
      ...日出世

In colloquial speech, sometimes the word for 'day', *yāt*, will be deleted.

15 August   *bāat yűet sāp nğ*   八月十五
      August 15

Festivals & Holidays

The Chinese New Year is the most celebrated festival for the Cantonese. In Hong Kong and Macau Christmas and Easter holidays are celebrated enthusiastically too. Of course, Valentine's Day, Father's Day, Mother's Day and International May Day are also in everyone's calendar.

The following Chinese traditional festivals are also well known in this area.

Chinese New Year   *nung lĭk sàn nin*   農曆新年

Lunar New Year, the most important festival in the year. The most common New Year greeting word is 'kung hei fat choy' *gùng héi fāat choi,* meaning 'everyone gains a lot of money'. A special New Year Eve's market, *nin sìu sǐ cheung,* is held every year in different suburbs in Hong Kong.

Qingming   *chìng míng*   清明

    Qingming means 'clear and bright', held on 4 or 5 April in the solar calendar. Together with the *chung yéung*, these are the two special days when the Chinese people sweep and tidy up their ancestors' tombs.

Dragon Boat Festival   *dùen ńg*   端午

    This is a day to celebrate the poet *wàt yuen,* who lived in the fourth century BC, during the Warring Kingdoms, in the country of *chóh*. It takes place on 5 May of the lunar calendar (late May to June in the solar calendar).

Maidens' Festival   *chàt jīk*   七夕

    The double seven (7 lunar July) festival is the day for young women. The Spinster Maid, *jīk nûi* (Vega) and her lover, the Cowboy, *ngau long* (Altair) are allowed to meet once only, on this eve.

Mid-Autumn Festival   *jùng chàu*   中秋

    Also known as Autumn Moon Festival, or Lantern Festival, it occurs on the full moon evening in lunar August. On this day everyone eats sweet moon cakes and some areas hold the lantern parade, especially for the children's entertainment.

chung yéung or *chung gáu*   重陽, 重九

    The double nine (9 lunar September) festival is the day for hiking and the sweeping of tombs.

Numbers & Amounts

Cardinal Numbers

The simplest way to make long numbers is to disregard the units of tens, hundreds and thousands, and use only the numbers from zero to nine. That means that for the number 1997, instead of *yàt chìn gáu bāak gáu sǎp chàt* (one thousand nine hundred ninety seven) you may just use *yàt gáu gáu chàt* (one nine nine seven).

0	*ling*	零
1	*yàt*	一
2	*yī* (or *léung**)	二（兩）
3	*sàam*	三
4	*sēi*	四
5	*ńg*	五
6	*lŭk*	六
7	*chàt*	七
8	*bāat*	八
9	*gáu*	九
10	*sǎp*	十

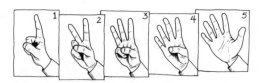

11	*sǎp yàt*	十一
12	*sǎp yī*	十二
13	*sǎp sàam*	十三
14	*sǎp sēi*	十四
15	*sǎp ńg*	十五
16	*sǎp lūk*	十六
17	*sǎp chàt*	十七
18	*sǎp bāat*	十八
19	*sǎp gáu*	十九
20	*yī sǎp*	二十
21	*yī sǎp yàt*	二十一
22	*yī sǎp yī*	二十二
23	*yī sǎp sàam*	二十三
29	*yī sǎp gáu*	二十九
30	*sàam sǎp*	三十
39	*sàam sǎp gáu*	三十九
40	*sēi sǎp*	四十
50	*ńg sǎp*	五十
60	*lūk sǎp*	六十
70	*chàt sǎp*	七十
80	*bāat sǎp*	八十
90	*gáu sǎp*	九十
99	*gáu sǎp gáu*	九十九
100	*yàt bāak*	一百
101	*yàt bāak ling yàt*	一百零一
110	*yàt bāak yàt sǎp*	一百一十
113	*yàt bāak yàt sǎp sàam*	一百一十三
120	*yàt bāak yī sǎp*	一百二十
190	*yàt bāak gáu sǎp*	一百九十
200	*yī bāak*	二佰

347	*sàam bāak sēi sǎp chàt*	三百四十七
999	*gáu bāak gáu sǎp gáu*	九百九十九
1000	*yàt chìn*	一千
1001	*yàt chìn ling yàt*	一千零一
9360	*gáu chìn sàam bāak lūk sǎp*	九千三百六十
10,000	*yàt mǎan*	一萬
100,000	*sǎp mǎan*	十萬
112,000	*sǎp yàt mǎan yī chìn*	十一萬二千
one million	*yàt bāak mǎan*	一百萬
1,230,000	*yàt bāak yī sǎp sàam mǎan*	一百二十三萬
10 million	*yàt chìn mǎan*	一千萬
100 million	*yàt yìk*	一億

* Another method of saying two is *léung,* which only applies to a single unit or classified units, and is used only in quantities.

2	*léung*	兩
20,000	*léung mǎan*	兩萬
2 sheets of paper	*léung jèung jí*	兩張紙
2 cups of tea	*léung bòoi cha*	兩杯茶

Measure Words

Measure words (classifiers) are normally necessary between numbers and countable nouns. There are hundreds of measure words, most of which refer to the noun's shape or appearance. The most common one is *gōh,* meaning 'a piece'; but it can also apply to people as well.

a basket	*lung*	籠
a bottle	*jùn*	樽
flat shape	*jèung*	張
long shape	*tiu*	條
pair	*dūi*	對

(2) baskets of barbecue pork buns
(*léung*) *lung chà sìu bàau*   兩籠叉燒飽

each table is for four (people).
sēi gōh yan yàt jèung tói   四個人一張枱

Decimal Point

Decimal point
... *dím* ...   ...點...

0.0023	*ling dím ling ling yī sàam*	零點零零二三
3.1416	*sàam dím yàt sēi yàt lūk*	三點一四一六
25.78	*yī sǎp ńg dím chàt bāat*	二十五點七八

Minus

Put the word *fǒo* in front of the figure to make it negative.

| minus ... | *fǒo* ... | 負... |
| -18.9 | *fǒo sǎp bāat dím gáu* | 負十八點九 |

Fractions

Unlike the Western way of looking at a fraction, that is, as one on three for a third, the Chinese see it as 'three parts one'. So to say a fraction, you should first say the denominator (in this case, three), followed by ... *fān jì* ..., then the numerator (one). For example,

⅓	*sàam fān jì yàt*	三分之一
²²⁄₇	*chàt fān jì yī sǎp yī*	七分之二十二

In the case of a mixed fraction, you first say the whole number, then add the word *yǎu*, then the rest will follow the above rule.

3¼	*sàam yǎu sēi fān jì yàt*	三又四分之一

Percentage

Simply add the numbers after the word 'percentage', *bāak fān jì*.

10%	*bāak fān jì sǎp*	百分之十
36.7%	*bāak fān jì sàam sǎp lūk dím chàt*	百分之三十六點七
-20%	*fōo bāak fān jì yī sǎp*	負百分之二十

When talking about a discount, the number applies to the amount paid rather than the amount being taken off. For example, instead of saying 15% off, the Cantonese say 85%.

10% discount = 90%	*gáu jǐt*	九折
15% discount = 85%	*bāat nǧ jǐt*	八五折

Ordinal Numbers

Add the word *dāi* before the cardinal numbers.

1st	*dāi yàt*	第一
2nd	*dāi yī*	第二
9th	*dāi gáu*	第九
23rd	*dāi yī sǎp sàam*	第二十三

the last	*dāi mèi*	第尾
the last one	*dō só dāi yàt*	倒數第一
the last two	*dō só dāi yī*	倒數第二

Units

Besides the metric system, the traditional Chinese system is also very common in daily life, especially in the local markets.

Metric System

km	*gùng léi*	公里
metre	*gùng chēk*	公尺
cm	*gùng fàn*	公分

My height is (182) cm.

ngőh sàn gò (yàt bāak bāat sǎp yī)	我身高(一百八十二)
gùng fàn	公分

kg	*gùng gàn*	公斤
gram	*hàk*	克
litre	*gùng sìng*	公升

Other Systems

yard	*mǎ*	碼
foot	*yìng chēk*	英呎
inch	*yìng chūen*	英吋
pound	*bõng*	磅
ounce	*ngòn sí*	安士
square foot	*fòng chēk*	方呎
the Chinese catty	*gàn*	斤
the Chinese tael	*léung*	两

3 catties equal 4 pounds (nearly 2 kg).
 sàam gàn dáng yùe sēi bõng 三斤等於四磅
16 taels equal a catty.
 sǎp lūk léung dáng yùe yàt gàn 十六两等於一斤

Amounts

dollar (formal)	*yuen*	元
dollar (general)	*màn*	文
dollar (colloquial)	... *gōh* ...	...個...
ten cents (formal)	*gōk*	角
ten cents (general & colloquial)	*ho jí*	毫子
a cent	*fàn*	分
a cent (general & colloquial)	*sìn*	仙
50 cents	*ng̃ ho jí*	五毫子
US dollar	*měi gàm*	美金
UK pounds	*yìng bóng*	英鎊
Australian dollar	*ngōu yuen*	澳元
Hong Kong dollar	*góng bãi*	港幣
Renminbi	*yan man bãi*	人民幣

Formal

The formal words are used for writing, formal reports, and so on.

US$24.60	*méi gàm yǐ sǎp sēi yuen lūk gōk*	美金二十四元六角
HK$1.38	*góng bǎi yàt yuen sàam gōk bāat fàn*	港幣一元三角八分
RMB$1.5	*yan man bǎi yàt yuen ńg gōk*	人民幣一元伍角

General

The general usage is for daily, casual conversation.

US$24.60	*méi gàm yǐ sǎp sēi màn lūk ho*	美金二十四文六毫
HK$1.38	*góng bǎi yàt màn sàam ho bāat sìn*	港幣一文三毫八仙
RMB$1.50	*yan man bǎi yàt màn ńg ho*	人民幣一文五毫

Colloquial

The colloquial usage takes place in price negotiations – at the market, for instance.

US$24.60	*méi gàm yǎ sēi gōh lūk*	美金廿四個六
HK$1.38	*góng bǎi yàt gōh sàam ho bāat*	港幣一個三毫八
RMB$1.50	*yan man bǎi gōh bōon*	人民幣個半

Some Useful Words

three-quarters	*sàam gōh gwàt*	三個骨
a lot/much	*hó dòh*	好多
a pair	*yàt dūi*	一對
a quarter	*yàt gōh gwàt*	一個骨
about	*dāai yēuk*	大約
add	*gà*	加
amount	*ngan mǎ*	銀碼
calculate	*gāi sō*	計數
count	*só*	數
divide	*chui*	除
double	*sèung pőoi*	雙倍
few	*ho síu*	好少
first time	*dāi yàt chī*	第一次
half	*yàt bōon*	一半
half price	*bōon gā*	半價
How many?	*géi dòh*	幾多
How much?	*géi dòh chín*	幾多錢
less	*síu*	少
more	*dòh*	多
multiply	*sing*	乘
number	*sō mūk*	數目
once	*yàt chī*	一次
subtract	*gáam*	減
triple	*sàam pőoi*	三倍
twice	*léung chi*	兩次

Vocabulary

A

address	*dĕi jí*	地址
admission fee	*yăp cheung fāi*	入場費
afraid	*pā*	怕
after ...	*... jì hāu*	...之後
agree	*tung yī*	同意
airmail	*hùng yau*	空郵
air pollution	*hùng hēi wòo yĭm*	空氣污染
airport	*gèi cheung*	機場
alarm clock	*năau jùng*	鬧鐘
alcohol	*jáu jìng*	酒精
always	*seng yăt*	成日
amount	*ngan mă*	銀碼
and	*tung maai*	同埋
angry	*nàu*	嬲
animals	*dŭng măt*	動物
area code	*dĕi kùi jĭ tau*	地區字頭
arrive	*dō dāat*	到達
ashtray	*yìn fòoi gòng*	煙灰缸

B

baby food	*yìng yi sĭk bán*	嬰兒食品
baby powder	*yìng yi sóng sàn fán*	嬰兒爽身粉
bad	*m hó*	唔好
baker	*mĭn bàau pó*	麵包舖
ballpoint pen	*yuen jí bàt*	原子筆
bamboo	*jùk*	竹

bank	*ngan hong*	銀行
banyan tree	*yung sūe*	榕樹
bar	*jáu bà*	酒吧
barber	*fèi fāat pó*	飛髮舖
beach	*sà tàan*	沙灘
bean sprouts	*nga chōi*	芽菜
before ...	*... jì chin*	...之前
beggar	*hàt yì*	乞兒
behind	*hău bīn*	後便
bicycle	*dàan chè*	單車
big	*dăai*	大
bill (check)	*dàan*	單
birds (long tail)	*nĭu*	鳥
birds (short tail)	*jēuk*	雀
birthday	*sàang yăt*	生日
black	*hàk*	黑
black market	*hàk sí*	黑市
blanket	*mo jìn*	毛氈
blood transfusion	*sùe hūet*	輸血
blue	*laam*	藍
book (n)	*sùe*	書
booking	*yūe yēuk*	預約
bookshop	*sùe gúk*	書局
boring	*mŏon*	悶
borrow	*jē*	借
botanical garden	*jīk măt yuen*	植物園
boyfriend	*naam pang yău*	男朋友
bread	*mĭn bàau*	麵飽
bridge	*kiu*	橋
brown	*fè sìk*	啡色
bucket	*túng*	桶

bus stop	*bà sí jăam*	巴士站
bus terminal	*bà sí júng jăam*	巴士總站
bus (in China)	*gùng gŭng hēi chè*	公共汽車
bus (Hong Kong)	*bà sí*	巴士
business class	*sèung mŏ hāk wái*	商務客位
businessperson	*sèung yan*	商人
button	*náu*	鈕

C

cake	*sài béng*	西餅
calculator	*gāi sō gèi*	計數機
camera	*séung gèi*	相機
cancel	*chúi sìu*	取消
cancer	*ngaam*	癌
candle	*lāap jùk*	蠟燭
canteen	*fāan tong*	飯堂
Cantonese food	*gwóng dùng chōi*	廣東菜
Cantonese (language)	*gwóng dùng wá*	廣東話
Cantonese (people)	*gwóng dùng yan*	廣東人
cap	*tàai yeung mó*	太陽帽
car park	*ting chè cheung*	停車場
cash	*yĭn gàm*	現金
cashmere	*kè sĭ mè*	茄士咩
cassette tape	*kà sìk lŭk yàm dáai*	卡式錄音帶
century	*sāi géi*	世紀
chair	*dāng*	櫈
cheap	*peng*	平
Cheers!	*gòn bòoi*	干杯
chef	*chue sì*	廚師
chemist	*yĕuk jài sì*	藥劑師

cheque	*jì pīu*	支票
cherry blossom	*yìng fà*	櫻花
child/children	*sāi ló gòh*	細路哥
chilli	*lăat jiu*	辣椒
chilli sauce	*lăat jiu jēung*	辣椒醬
China	*jùng gwōk*	中國
Chinese food	*jùng gwōk chōi*	中國菜
Chinese herbal tea	*leung cha*	涼茶
Chinese restaurant	*jáu lau*	酒樓
Chinese tea	*jùng gwōk cha*	中國茶
Chinese tea house	*cha lau*	茶樓
Chinese wine	*jùng gwōk jáu*	中國酒
chopsticks	*fāai jí*	筷子
cigarette	*yìn jái*	煙仔
circus	*mă hēi*	馬戲
city	*sìng sí*	城市
Clag paste	*jèung woo*	漿糊
clam	*pŏng*	蚌
classical music	*góo dín yàm ngŏk*	古典音樂
clothing	*yì fŭk*	衣服
coat	*ngŏi tō*	外套
coffee	*gā fè*	咖啡
coffee house	*gā fè tèng*	咖啡廳
cold	*dūng*	凍
cold water	*dūng súi*	凍水
collect call	*dūi fòng fŏo fóon dĭn wá*	對方付款電話
colour	*chói sìk*	彩色
comb	*sòh*	梳
computer	*dĭn nŏ*	電腦
condoms	*bĕi yăn tō*	避孕套

confirm	*kōk yīng*	確認
Congratulations!	*gùng hēi*	恭喜
copy machine	*yíng yān gèi*	影印機
correction fluid	*gói chōh súi*	改錯水
cotton	*min*	棉
count	*só*	數
countryside	*gàau ngòi*	郊外
country (ph) code	*gwōk gà pìn hõ*	國家編號
country park	*gàau yé gùng yúen*	郊野公園
credit card	*sūn yúng kàat*	信用卡
cup	*bòoi*	杯
curry	*gā lèi*	咖喱
customs	*hói gwàan*	海關
customs declaration	*hói gwàan sàn bō dàan*	海關申報單

D

dancing	*tīu mó*	跳舞
date of birth	*chùt sàng nin yúet yàt*	出生年月日
daughter	*núi*	女
day	*yàt*	日
delicious	*hó sīk*	好食
dental floss	*nga sīn*	牙線
deodorant	*chui chāu jài*	除臭劑
depart	*chùt fāat*	出發
department store	*bāak fōh gùng sì*	百貨公司
departure	*chùt gíng*	出境
dictionary	*jī dín*	字典
direct dial	*jīk bõot dīn wá*	直撥電話
direction	*fòng hēung*	方向

directory	*dīn wá bó*	電話部
discount	*jīt tau*	折頭
doctor	*yì sàng*	醫生
dolls	*gùng jái*	公仔
double	*sèung pőoi*	雙倍
down	*hă bīn*	下便
dozen	*dà*	打
dress	*tō jòng*	套裝
dress shop	*sìng yì dīm*	成衣店
driver	*sì gèi*	司機
driving licence	*chè paai*	車牌
duty free shop	*mĭn sūi dīm*	免稅店

E

early	*jó*	早
earrings	*yĭ wáan*	耳環
economy class	*gìng jāi wái*	經濟位
enough	*gāu*	夠
entertainment	*sìu hín*	消遣
envelope	*sūn fùng*	信封
every day	*mőoi yăt*	每日
exchange (money)	*jáau wŏon*	找換
expensive	*gwāi*	貴
express mail	*fāai yau*	快郵
express train	*dăk fāai*	特快

F

far away	*yűen*	遠
fast train	*fāai chè*	快車
father	*fŏo chàn*	父親
fax	*chuen jàn*	傳眞

fax machine	*chuen jàn gèi*	傳眞機
ferry	*dõ hói síu lun*	渡海小輪
ferry pier	*síu lun mã tau*	小輪碼頭
file	*man gín gáap*	文件夾
film	*fèi lám*	菲林
first	*dãi yàt*	第一
first class	*tau dáng*	頭等
fish	*yúe*	魚
fisher	*yue fòo*	漁夫
flight number ...	*... hõ bàan gèi*	...號班機
floating restaurant	*hói sìn fóng*	海鮮舫
florist	*fà dìm*	花店
flower	*fà*	花
food street	*sĩk gàai*	食街
forever	*wĩng yũen*	永遠
forget-me-not	*mo mong ngõh*	毋忘我
formal wear	*lãi fũk*	禮服
fountain	*pān chuen*	噴泉
fresh	*sàn sìn*	新鮮
fresh juice	*sìn gwóh jàp*	鮮果汁
fried noodles	*chàau mĩn*	炒麵
fried rice	*cháau fãan*	炒飯
friend	*pang yũu*	朋友
fruit	*sàang gwóh*	生果
fruit juice	*gwóh jàp*	果汁
fruit salad	*jãap gwóh sà lũt*	雜果沙律

G

garden	*fà yúen*	花園
gate (boarding)	*dàng gèi jãap háu*	登機閘口
girlfriend	*nũi pang yũu*	女朋友

give way	*yĕung lŏ*	讓路
glasses	*ngăan géng*	眼鏡
gloves	*sáu tō*	手套
gold	*gàm*	金
good	*hó*	好
government	*jīng fóo*	政府
grandfather	*jó fŏo*	祖父
grandmother	*jó mŏ*	祖母
grass	*chó*	草
green	*lũk*	綠
green tea	*lũk cha*	綠茶
grocery	*jăap fōh pó*	雜貨舖
guest	*yan hāak*	人客
gum tree	*jeŭng gàau sũe*	橡膠樹

H

hair	*tau fāat*	頭髮
hairbrush	*sòh*	梳
half	*yàt bōon*	一半
handbag	*sáu dói*	手袋
handmade	*sáu gùng jŏ*	手工造
handerchief	*sáu gàn*	手巾
happy	*hòi sàm*	開心
harbour	*góng háu*	港口
heavy	*chŭng*	重
herbal tea	*leung cha*	涼茶
here	*nì dŏ*	呢度
highway	*gùng lŏ*	公路
historical sites	*góo jìk*	古跡
homemaker	*júe fŏo*	主婦
hot	*yīt*	熱

hour	*jùng tau*	鐘頭
How many?	*géi dòh?*	幾多
How much?	*géi dòh chín?*	幾多錢
hungry	*ngōh*	餓
husband	*jĕung fòo*	丈夫
husband (colloquial)	*lŏ gùng*	老公

I

ice cream	*sūet gò*	雪糕
identification card	*sàn fán jīng*	身份証
in front of ...	*... chìn bīn*	...前便
inside	*lŭi bīn*	裡便
international call	*gwōk jāi dīn wá*	國際電話
interpreter	*fàan yĭk*	翻譯
interval	*bōon cheung yàu sìk*	半場休息
invoice	*fāat pīu*	發票
itinerary	*hang chìng bíu*	行程表

J

jogging	*páau bŏ*	跑步
journalist	*gēi jé*	記者

K

kangaroo	*dŏi súe*	袋鼠
kiosk	*síu sĭk dīm*	小食店
kiss	*mán*	吻
knife and fork	*dò chà*	刀叉

L

last night	*kam mǎan*	噚晚
late	*chi dō*	遲到
laundry	*sái yì pó*	洗衣舖
lawyer	*lūt sì*	律師
leather	*péi*	皮
leave	*lei hòi*	離開
lecturer	*góng sì*	講師
left	*jóh bìn*	左便
less	*síu*	少
library	*to sùe gwóon*	圖書館
light	*hèng*	輕
light-train stop	*hìng tīt jǎam*	輕鐵站
lighter	*dá fóh gèi*	打火機
like	*jùng yī*	中意
local call	*sí nǒi dǐn wá*	市內電話
long	*cheung*	長
long-distance bus station	*cheung to hēi chè jǎam*	長途汽車站
long-distance call	*cheung to dǐn wá*	長途電話
lookout	*liu mǒng toi*	瞭望臺
lotus	*hoh fà*	荷花
lotus root	*lin ngǎu*	蓮藕
lotus seed	*lin jí*	蓮子
lounge	*jáu long*	酒廊

M

magazine	*jǎap jǐ*	雜誌
mahjong (to play)	*dá ma jēuk*	麻雀

manager	*gìng léi*	經理
map	*déi to*	地圖
marker	*sèung tau bàt*	箱頭筆
massage	*ngōn mòh*	按摩
matches	*fóh chaai*	火柴
mattress	*chong jín*	床墊
midnight	*bōon yé*	半夜
mineral water	*kwōng chuen súi*	礦泉水
minibus	*síu bà*	小巴
minus	*fōo*	負
minute	*fàn*	分
mirror	*gēng*	鏡
mobile phone	*dāai gòh dāai*	大哥大
money exchange	*jáau wǒon dīm*	找換店
moon	*yǔet*	月
mother	*mǒ chàn*	母親
motorbike	*dīn dàan chè*	電單車
music	*yàm ngǒk*	音樂
musical instruments	*ngǒk hēi*	樂器

N

name	*sīng ming*	姓名
napkin	*jí gàn*	紙巾
nationality	*gwōk jīk*	國籍
never	*chung loi mǒ*	從來冇
newspaper	*bō jí*	報紙
next month	*hǎ gōh yǔet*	下個月
noisy	*cho*	嘈
number	*sō mǔk*	數目
nurse	*wǒo sī*	護士

O

occupation	*jìk yīp*	職業
... o'clock	*... dím*	...點
old friend	*ló yáu*	老友
once	*yàt chī*	一次
operator	*jīp sīn sàng*	接線生
opposite (side)	*dùi mìn*	對面

P

padlock	*sóh tau*	鎖頭
panda	*hung màau*	熊貓
paper	*jí*	紙
parking service	*dõi hāak pāak chè*	代客泊車
passport	*wõo jīu*	護照
passport number	*wõo jīu hõ má*	護照號碼
pencil	*yuen bàt*	鉛筆
perfume	*hèung súi*	香水
pharmacy	*yēuk fong*	藥房
photo	*sēung pín*	相片
physiotherapist	*màt léi jī liu sì*	物理治療師
pipe	*yìn dáu*	煙斗
place of birth	*chùt sàng dēi*	出生地
plate	*dīp*	碟
plug	*chāap táu*	插頭
poisonous snake	*dūk se*	毒蛇
policeman		
(in China)	*gùng ngòn*	公安
(in Hong Kong)	*gíng chāat*	警察
poplar	*bãak yeung sūe*	白楊樹
popular music	*lau hang yàm ngõk*	流行音樂

pork	*jùe yūk*	豬肉
postcard	*mìng sūn pín*	明信片
postman	*yau chàai*	郵差
post office	*yau gúk*	郵局
pot	*woo*	壺
printed matter	*yān chāat bán*	印刷品
profession	*jùen yĩp*	專業
public telephone	*gùng jūng dĩn wá*	公眾電話
public toilet	*gùng chĩ*	公廁
pull	*làai*	拉
push	*tùi*	推

Q

quarantine	*gím yĩk*	檢疫

R

radio	*sàu yàm gèi*	收音機
railway station	*fóh chè jāam*	火車站
raincoat	*yũe yì*	雨衣
raw fish	*yue sàang*	魚生
razor	*tāi dò*	剃刀
reading	*tái sùe*	睇書
receipt	*sàu gūi*	收據
recently	*jūi gǎn*	最近
red	*hung*	紅
registered mail	*gwā hŏ sūn*	掛號信
relatives	*chàn chìk*	親戚
religion	*jùng gāau*	宗教
restaurant	*chàan tèng*	餐廳
restricted area	*gām kùi*	禁區
return call	*fùk dĩn wá*	覆電話

rice (cooked)	*fāan*	飯
rice bowl	*fāan wóon*	飯碗
ricefield	*dō tin*	稻田
rickshaw	*chè jái*	車仔
right	*yāu bìn*	右便
ring	*gāai jí*	戒指
road	*dō lō*	道路
rock	*ngaam sēk*	岩石
rubbish	*lāap sāap*	垃圾
rubbish bin	*lāap sāap túng*	垃圾桶

S

sad	*sèung sàm*	傷心
safe/safety box	*bó hím sèung*	保險箱
safety pin	*kāu jàm*	扣針
salt	*yim*	鹽
sandals	*leung haai*	涼鞋
sandwich	*sàam man jī*	三文治
sanitary napkins	*wāi sàng gàn*	衛生巾
scared	*gèng*	驚
scientist	*fòh hōk gà*	科學家
scissors	*gāau jín*	較剪
scoop (for rice)	*faan hōk*	飯殼
scoop (for soup)	*tòng gàng*	湯羹
screwdriver	*loh sì pài*	螺絲批
sea	*hói*	海
seafood restaurant	*hói sìn jáu gà*	海鮮酒家
seasons	*gwāi jīt*	季節
seaweed	*jí chōi*	紫菜
second (adj)	*dāi yī*	第二
second (time)	*míu*	秒

secretary	*bēi sùe*	秘書
section	*fàn dǔen*	分段
self-adhesive labels	*yǐ tīp bìu chìm*	自貼標簽
service charge	*fūk mǒ fāi*	服務費
shame	*cháu*	醜
shampoo	*sái tau súi*	洗頭水
sharpener	*yuen bàt páau*	鉛筆刨
shirt	*sùt sàam*	裇衫
shoe polish	*haai yáu*	鞋油
shoes	*haai*	鞋
shop	*pō táu*	舖頭
short	*dúen*	短
signature	*chìm méng*	簽名
silk	*sì*	絲
silver	*ngan*	銀
single	*dàan sàn*	單身
skirt	*kwan*	裙
sleepy	*ngǎan fān*	眼瞓
small	*sāi*	細
smells nice	*hó hèung*	好香
soap	*fàan gáan*	番梘
social dance	*gàau jāi mǒ*	交際舞
socks	*mǎt*	襪
soft drink	*hēi súi*	汽水
soldier	*gwàn yan*	軍人
son	*jái*	仔
soup	*tòng*	湯
spoon	*chi gàng*	匙羹
sport	*wǎn dǔng*	運動
sportswear	*wǎn dǔng jòng*	運動裝

spring	*chùn gwāi*	春季
stamps	*yau pīu*	郵票
stapler	*dèng sùe gèi*	釘書機
star	*sìng*	星
sticky tape	*gàau jí*	膠紙
stockings	*sì mǎt*	絲襪
stop	*ting*	停
student	*hǒk sàang*	學生
subtract	*gáam*	減
suburb	*sí gàau*	市郊
subway station	*dēi tīt jǎam*	地鐵站
sun	*yǎt táu* or	日頭
	tāai yeung	太陽
sunblock cream	*tāai yeung yau*	太陽油
sunglasses	*tāai yeung ngǎan géng*	太陽眼鏡
superhighway	*chìu kàp gùng lǒ*	超級公路
supermarket	*chìu kàp sí cheung*	超級市場
swimming	*yau súi*	游水
swimming suit	*yau wǐng yì*	游泳衣

T

table	*tói*	枱
tablecloth	*tói bō*	枱布
tall	*gò*	高
taxi stand	*dìk sí jǎam*	的士站
tea	*cha*	茶
tea with milk	*nǎi cha*	奶茶
teacher	*gāau sì*	教師
teapot	*cha wóo*	茶壺
teaspoon	*cha gàng*	茶羹

technician	*gĕi gùng*	技工
telegram	*dĭn bō*	電報
telephone	*dĭn wá*	電話
telephone booth	*dĭn wá ting*	電話亭
telephone card	*dĭn wá kàat*	電話卡
telephone number	*dĭn wá hŏ má*	電話號碼
temple	*míu*	廟
that	*góh gōh*	嗰個
there	*góh dŏ*	嗰度
thirsty	*háu hōt*	口渴
this	*nì gōh*	呢個
ticket	*fèi*	飛
ticket office	*său pīu chŭe*	售票處
tie	*tàai*	呔
timetable	*si gāan bíu*	時間表
tip (payment)	*tìp sí*	貼士
tired	*gwŏoi*	攰
tissues	*jí gàn*	紙巾
tobacco	*yìn sì*	煙絲
today	*gàm yăt*	今日
toilet	*chī sóh*	廁所
toilet paper	*chī jí*	廁紙
tomorrow	*tìng yăt*	聽日
tonight	*gàm màan*	今晚
toothbrush	*nga cháat*	牙刷
toothpaste	*nga gò*	牙膏
toothpick	*nga chìm*	牙簽
torch (flashlight)	*sáu dĭn túng*	手電筒
tourist	*yau hāak*	遊客
tower	*tāap*	塔
toys	*wŏon gŭi*	玩具

traffic jam	*sàt chè*	塞車
train	*fóh chè*	火車
train station	*fóh chè jǎam*	火車站
tram stop	*dīn chè jǎam*	電車站
tramways	*dīn chè*	電車
transit	*jūen gèi*	轉機
trash	*lǎap sāap*	垃圾
travellers' cheque	*lǘi hang jì pīu*	旅行支票
travelling	*lǘi hang*	旅行
tray	*poon*	盤
tree	*sūe*	樹
triple	*sàam pǒoi*	三倍
tripod	*sàam gēuk gá*	三腳架
trousers	*fōo*	褲
T-shirt	*T-sùt*	T-袖
TV	*dīn sī*	電視
twice	*léung chi*	兩次
typewriter	*dá jī gèi*	打字機
typhoon	*gǔi fùng*	颶風
tyre	*chè tàai*	車胎

U

uncle	*sùk sùk*	叔叔
university	*dāai hǒk*	大學
up	*sēung bīn*	上便
upgrade ticket	*bó pīu*	補票

V

vaseline	*fà sī líng*	花士令
vegetable	*sòh chōi*	蔬菜

vegetarian food	*jàai chōi*	齋菜
video camera	*síp lūk gèi*	攝錄機
video tape	*lūk yíng dáai*	錄影帶
village	*hèung chùen*	鄉村
visa	*chìm jĭng*	簽証

W

waiter (f)	*síu jé*	小姐
waiter (m)	*fóh gēi*	伙記
waiting room (airport)	*hău gèi sàt*	侯機室
wasabi	*yāt bóon gāai lāat*	日本芥辣
watch	*sáu bìu*	手錶
water	*súi*	水
week	*sìng kei*	星期
well (adj)	*hó*	好
Western food	*sài chàan*	西餐
Western-style restaurant	*sài chàan tèng*	西餐廳
wet towel	*sàp mo gàn*	濕毛巾
white	*bāak*	白
wife	*tāai táai*	太太
wife (colloquial)	*lŏ pŏh*	老婆
wool	*mo*	毛
worried	*dàam sàm*	擔心
writing brush	*mo bàt*	毛筆

Y

yellow	*wong*	黃
yesterday	*kam yāt*	噖日
younger brother	*dai dái*	弟弟

| younger sister | *mooi móoi* | 妹妹 |
| yum cha | *yám cha* | 飲茶 |

Z

zebra crossing	*bàan mǎ sīn*	斑馬線
zipper	*làai lín*	拉鍊
zoo	*dǒng màt yuen*	動物園

Tiger

Emergencies

In Hong Kong, the phone number 999, *gáu gáu gáu*, serves all emergencies while in Macau, 333 is for the police and 3300 for an ambulance. The Public Security Bureau (PSB), *gùng ngòn,* is China's police force, and their foreign affairs departments, *ngõi sī fòh,* take care of foreigners, including applications for visa extension. Check the telephone number of your embassy or consulate in case of an emergency.

Shout the following words in case of an emergency. The most common word is *gāu mẽng ā!* literally meaning 'save my life', or 'help!'.

Help!	*gāu mẽng ā!*	救命呀!
fire	*fóh jùk ā*	火燭呀
thief	*chéung yé ā*	搶嘢呀
Catch him!	*jùk jūe kúi*	捉住佢
Be careful!	*síu sàm*	小心
Danger!	*ngai hím*	危險
Don't move!	*mãi yùk*	咪郁
Go away!	*jáu hòi*	走開
Stop!	*ting dài*	停低
Watch out!	*síu sàm*	小心

Reporting an Accident

There's been an accident!
  góh dõ fāat sàng yī ngõi 嗰度發生意外

There's been a collision!
  góh dõ jõng chè 嗰度撞車

There's a fight.
  yáu yan dá gàau   有人打交
Someone has been injured.
  yáu yan sāu sèung   有人受傷

Victim

I have been injured.
  ngőh sāu jóh sèung   我受咗傷
I have been raped.
  ngőh bēi yan keung gàan   我被人強姦
I have been robbed.
  ngőh bēi yan dá gīp   我被人打劫
I have lost my ...
  ngőh m gīn jóh ngőh ge...   我唔見咗我嘅...
Someone took my ...
  yáu yan nìng jóh ngőh gē...   有人攞咗我嘅...

backpack	*bōoi nong*	背囊
bag	*dói*	袋
camera	*yíng séung gèi*	影相機
handbag	*sáu dói*	手袋
money	*chín*	錢
passport	*wŏo jīu*	護照
wallet	*ngan bàau*	銀包
watch	*sáu bìu*	手錶

Emergency Call

Call an ambulance!	*gīu gāu sèung chè*	叫救傷車
Call a doctor!	*gīu yì sàng*	叫醫生
Call the fire brigade!	*gīu sìu fong gúk*	叫消防局
Call the police!	*gīu gíng chāat*	叫警察
or (in China)	*gīu gùng ngòn*	叫公安

Needing Medical Attention

He/She needs a doctor.
  yīu bòng kúi gīu yì sàng
要幫佢叫醫生

He/She needs first aid.
  yīu bòng kúi gàp gāu
要幫佢急救

He/She needs to go to a hospital.
  yīu sūng kūi hūi yì yúen
要送佢去醫院

My blood group is (A, B, O, AB)
  positive/negative.
  ngőh gē hūet ying hāi (A, B, O, AB)
  ying jīng/főo
我嘅血型係
(A,B,O,AB)型正/負

Some Useful Phrases

Where is the toilet?
  chéng mǎn chī sóh hái bìn dő ā?
請問廁所喺邊度呀?

I am lost.
  ngőh dőng sàt jóh lő
我蕩失咗路

Could you help me please?
  hőh m hőh yí chéng nếi bòng sáu ā?
可唔可以請你幫手呀?

Can anyone speak English?
  yấu mő yan sìk gòng yìng mán
有冇人識講英文

Do you understand?
  ming m ming ā?
明唔明呀?

I understand.
  ngőh ming
我明

I don't understand.
  ngőh m ming
我唔明

I am terribly sorry.
  hó dūi m jűe
好對唔住

I did not do it.
  ngőh mő jő dő
我冇做到

Not me!
  m hãi ngốh!   唔係我

Could I please use the telephone?
  hóh m hóh yí dá gōh dĩn wá ā?   可唔可以打個電話呀

I wish to contact my ...
  ngốh séung tung ngốh gē ... luen lōk   我想同我嘅... 聯絡
    embassy   *dāai sī gwóon*   大使館
    consulate   *lĩng sī gwóon*   領事館
    family   *gà yan*   家人
    lawyer   *lũt sì*   律師

Some Useful Words

armed robbery	*dá gĩp*	打劫
crime	*jũi*	罪
emergency	*gán gàp*	緊急
fire engine	*gāu fóh chè*	救火車
first aid	*gàp gāau*	急救
hands up!	*gúi gò sáu*	舉高手
indecent assault	*fèi lái*	非禮
loss	*súen sàt*	損失
next of kin	*gà sũk*	家屬
pickpocket	*dá hoh bàau*	打荷包
quick	*fāai dì*	快啲
snatching	*chéung yế ā*	搶嘢呀
theft!	*tàu yế ā*	偷嘢呀
witness	*jĩng yan*	証人
wounded person	*sèung jé*	傷者
victim	*sãu hõi yan*	受害人

Language Survival Kits

Arabic (Egyptian) phrasebook

Arabic (Moroccan) phrasebook

Brazilian phrasebook

Burmese phrasebook

Cantonese phrasebook

Eastern Europe phrasebook
Covers Bulgarian, Czech, Hungarian, Polish, Romanian and Slovak.

Thai Hill Tribes phrasebook

Hindi/Urdu phrasebook

Indonesian phrasebook

Japanese phrasebook

Korean phrasebook

Mandarin Chinese phrasebook

Mediterranean Europe phrasebook
Covers Albanian, Greek, Italian, Macedonian, Maltese, Serbian & Croatian and Slovene.

Nepali phrasebook

Pidgin phrasebook

Pilipino phrasebook

Quechua phrasebook

Russian phrasebook

Scandinavian Europe phrasebook
Includes the following: Danish, Finnish, Icelandic, Norwegian and Swedish.

Spanish (Latin American) phrasebook

Sri Lanka phrasebook

Swahili phrasebook

Thai phrasebook

Tibet phrasebook

Turkish phrasebook

Vietnamese phrasebook

Western Europe phrasebook
Useful words and phrases in Basque, Catalan, Dutch, French, German, Irish, Portuguese, Spanish (Castilian).

LONELY PLANET PUBLICATIONS
Australia: PO Box 617, Hawthorn, Victoria 3122
USA: 155 Filbert Street, Suite 251, Oakland CA 94607-2538
UK: 10 Barley Mow Passage, Chiswick, London W4 4PH
France: 71 bis, rue du Cardinal Lemoine – 75005 Paris

Keep in touch!

We love hearing from you and think you'd like to hear from us.

The Lonely Planet newsletter covers the when, where, how and what of travel. (AND it's free!)

When...*is the right time to see reindeer in Finland?*
Where...*can you hear the best palm-wine music in Ghana?*
How...*do you get from Asunción to Areguá by steam train?*
What...*should you leave behind to avoid hassles with customs in Iran?*

To join our mailing list just contact us at any of our offices. (details below)

Every issue includes:

* *a letter from Lonely Planet founders Tony and Maureen Wheeler*
* *travel diary from a Lonely Planet author - find out what it's really like out on the road*
* *feature article on an important and topical travel issue*
* *a selection of recent letters from our readers*
* *the latest travel news from all over the world*
* *details on Lonely Planet's new and forthcoming releases*

Also available Lonely Planet T-Shirts. 100% heavy weight cotton (S, M, L, XL)

LONELY PLANET PUBLICATIONS
Australia: PO Box 617, Hawthorn, Victoria 3122 (tel: 03-819 1877)
USA: 155 Filbert Street, Suite 251, Oakland, CA 94607 (tel: 510-893 8555)
UK: 10 Barley Mow Passage, Chiswick, London W4 4PH (tel: 081-742 3161)
FRANCE: 71 bis, rue du Cardinal Lemoine – 75005 Paris